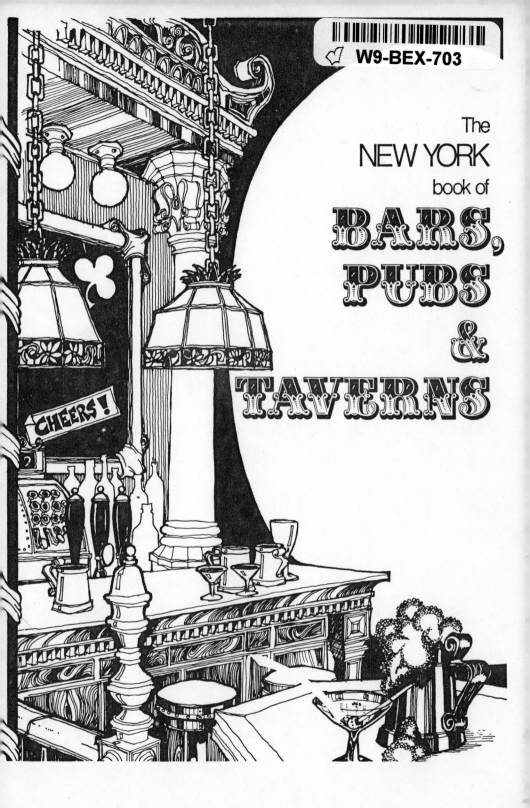

The
NEW YORK
book of
BARS,
PUBS
&
TAVERNS

CHEERS!

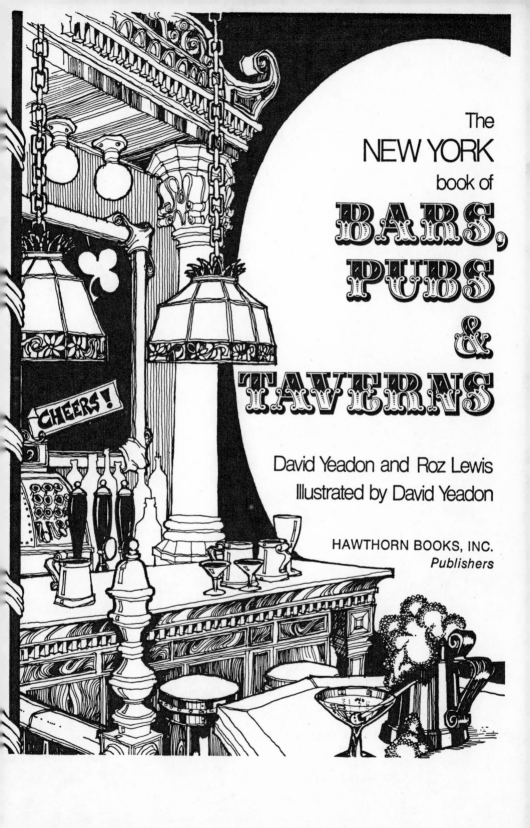

The
NEW YORK
book of
BARS,
PUBS
&
TAVERNS

David Yeadon and Roz Lewis
Illustrated by David Yeadon

HAWTHORN BOOKS, INC.
Publishers

CHEERS!

For Fereydoon and Elizabeth

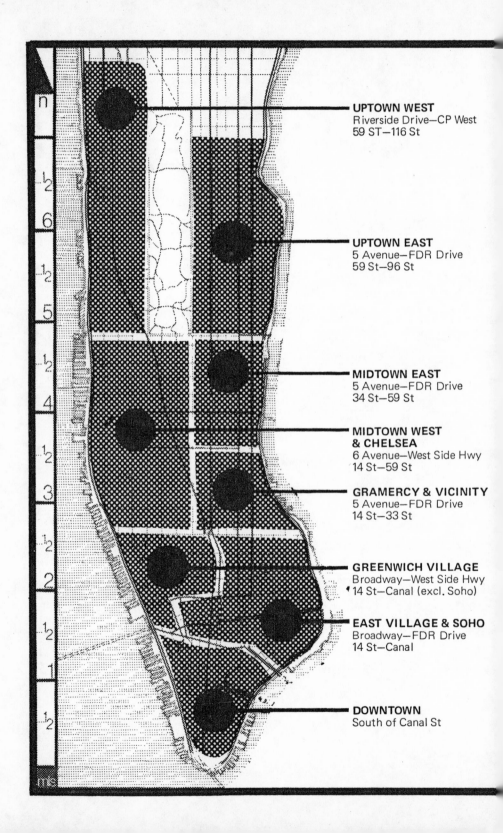

UPTOWN WEST
Riverside Drive—CP West
59 ST—116 St

UPTOWN EAST
5 Avenue—FDR Drive
59 St—96 St

MIDTOWN EAST
5 Avenue—FDR Drive
34 St—59 St

**MIDTOWN WEST
& CHELSEA**
6 Avenue—West Side Hwy
14 St—59 St

GRAMERCY & VICINITY
5 Avenue—FDR Drive
14 St—33 St

GREENWICH VILLAGE
Broadway—West Side Hwy
14 St—Canal (excl. Soho)

EAST VILLAGE & SOHO
Broadway—FDR Drive
14 St—Canal

DOWNTOWN
South of Canal St

CONTENTS

GREENWICH VILLAGE

And for your further enjoyment . . .

GRAMERCY AND VICINITY

And for your further enjoyment . . .

MIDTOWN WEST AND CHELSEA

And for your further enjoyment . . .

MIDTOWN EAST

And for your further enjoyment . . .

UPTOWN WEST

And for your further enjoyment . . .

UPTOWN EAST

And for your further enjoyment . . .

x

NEW YORK'S BARS, PUBS & TAVERNS

New York has the largest number and, without doubt, the finest variety of bars, pubs, and taverns of any city in the country. Even during the height of the Tory period, just prior to the Revolution, New York was the nightlife center of the emerging nation. British tavern-keepers, backed by centuries of experience in the homeland, ran highly regarded and reputable establishments with such stately titles as The Prince of Wales, The King's Arms, The Queen's Head, and The Lord Cornwallis.

Even following the Revolution, when most of the city's Royalists were obliged to make hasty exits, leaving behind their inns and taking with them only their experience, New York's taverns grew rapidly in number and popularity. Coffee houses, pleasure gardens, chop houses, lobster palaces, and elaborate restaurants emerged to serve the wealthier resident. Grog shops, gin mills, beer halls, concert saloons, dance houses, and oyster saloons satisfied the varied needs of the poorer immigrants and merchant seamen who, in their teeming thousands, filled the narrow streets and cramped tenements of the lower city.

During the nineteenth century the city grew at a staggering rate, moving ever northward up the island. Only the elite, the wealthiest of the citizens, could afford to live far up Fifth Avenue away from the hurley-burley. The remainder of the monied class were pursued relentlessly by tidal waves of newly arrived settlers—Irish, Italian, French, German, East European, and later Orientals—that gnawed, battered, and burst through the barriers of fashionable Georgian-styled streets in a relentless search for more space.

The same pattern continues today—although at a less pronounced pace and with more interesting repercussions. Manhattan is a jigsaw puzzle—a series of islands—of tiny contrasting communities. As E. B. White wrote in his delightful and perceptive essay "Here Is New York": "The curious thing about New York is that each large geographical unit is composed of countless smaller neighborhoods. Each neighborhood is self-sufficient. Each area is a city within a city within a city."

Each "city" today has its own distinct population and character, its own social norms and traditions and its own particular brand of bars, pubs, and taverns. The Village has its treasured literary enclaves; downtown its older, more traditional taverns; uptown east its singles bars catering to a bedroom population of young students and professionals; and Broadway its hallowed theatrical centuries.

Yet the city grows and changes. Soho, which only a few years ago was a murky district of tiny factories and warehouses, is emerging as Manhattan's new liberal and cultural center with its own particular form of local pubs. Uptown west is the "New Village" where old Irish saloons are being remodelled, brightened, and lightened to cater to the influx of twentieth-century bohemians. The Bowery is being revived as the new heart of off-Broadway theatre. And even the tradition-bound financial district around Wall Street is experiencing an imaginative new life. Many of the pubs and taverns here no longer close after the brief cocktail hour—some even romp on until the early hours of the morning, filled with the sounds of jazz or Irish music.

This book, therefore, is hopefully, more than merely an alphabetical guide to Manhattan's magnificent range of bars, pubs, and taverns. We have tried within its pages to give readers some insight into the history and traditions that lie behind these establishments in the belief that successful neighborhood pubs invariably reflect much about the area in which they are located and the people that lived and live there. Thus we modestly suggest that in order to fully appreciate and understand and enjoy the reviews in this book, readers should not overlook the descriptive summaries that precede the individual reviews in each of the neighborhood sections.

Our main hope, however, no matter how you use this book, is that you find fresh enjoyment in this great city and in its superb bars, pubs, and taverns.

SKETCHES AND LENGTH OF REVIEW

The length of review or the presence/absence of a sketch is in no way indicative of "rating." There is no star system in this book. All establishments included were selected on their own merits and in relation to their popularity. We've omitted places for which reviews would have been unfavorable. However, we may also have omitted worthy places unintentionally and welcome suggestions from readers for future revisions of this book.

The reviews in the "For Your Further Enjoyment" sections at the end of each chapter are relatively short, but again, this is not a reflection of rating. Many of these bars are already familiar to residents of Manhattan, and it has been our general intent to give prominence to less widely known establishments.

DOWNTOWN

John Gunther's famous comment on Manhattan—"It stays up all night"—hardly applies to the downtown area. With a few notable exceptions stores, pubs, and restaurants are closed and shuttered by 9 P.M.—a full hour or more before the city's nightlife begins in neighborhoods like the Village, Yorkville, or the upper west side. The streets, brooding and dark, are devoid of people and traffic. A few lights burn in the glass towers; the occasional resident (a rare sight indeed) scurries to some lonely loft; the sound of a ship's hooter echoes up the canyons.

What a contrast to the scene 100 years ago when great clippers lined the wharves along the East River. Markets and merchants operated twenty-four hours a day; the dockside taverns and dance houses were filled with a motley and boisterous selection of sailors and ladies of the night; gentlemen peered through the curtained windows of their clubs at the churning scene below; and elegant restaurants served the most exotic cuisines until the early hours of the morning. Those were the days when "downtown" was the city. Fortunate residents lived a little further uptown around Astor Place, Union Square, or in the great mansions that lined Fifth Avenue. But the majority—immigrants from Germany, Ireland, France, and the eastern European countries—were ghettoed around the markets on the lower east side or the ghastly Five-Points district at Park and Worth streets. This slum to end all slums was centered around a building known as the Old Brewery —the notorious crime headquarters of the city in which, during one survey, 1,200 people were classified as residents. Its nickname "Den of Thieves" was most appropriate. A nearby street labelled "Murderers' Alley" boasted the highest death rate in the city. According to nineteenth-century journalist James McCabe,

3

Jr., there was "scarcely a house without a distillery" (the term was used in its widest possible sense). Brothels, rum shops, and gin mills occupied every corner.

Gradually the city expanded northward, engulfing the palatial town houses of Union Square in its search for a new heart. Businesses left downtown, the newspaper offices left Printing House Square, great stores were opened up on 14th Street, then later 23rd Street, then 34th Street, and finally midtown. The port diminished in significance. Large draft ships could no longer negotiate the shallow, cramped wharves of the East River. The poorer residents moved north with the jobs, and downtown, while remaining an important financial center, lost much of its life and vigor.

David Rockefeller's 1955 decision to headquarter his Chase Manhattan Bank in a new sixty-story building on William Street helped turn the tide. Great glass and steel towers began to rise, overshadowing the old landmarks; even the Woolworth Building looked rather insignificant against the new skyline. Yet downtown remained very much a 9 to 5 district. The closure of the Washington Market in 1967 killed much of the tavern life on the west side downtown, and, unless the South Street renovation project materializes, the same will occur on the east side when the Fulton Fish Market moves out in 1976.

Yet all is not lost. Even though the alarming evening rush for the subways still leaves most taverns without customers after the cocktail hour, there has been a recent emergence of establishments whose owners are determined to re-create a night scene in, the area. Rosie O'Grady's South, an Irish pub with live entertainment, blasts along until 4 A.M. most nights of the week. Harry's (at Hanover Square) caters to an older business clientele, but still manages to attract a hearty patronage until after midnight. In similar fashion, The Atrium, St. Charlie's South, The Jolly Monk, Doyle's, Barnabus Rex, and Morgan's all keep their doors open long after most other places close. And each has its own distinct atmosphere and loyal clientele.

Of course, for most downtowners, particularly those with a one- to two-hour commute, lunch times and cocktail hours are the prime occasions for tavern patronage, and in this regard there are a host of splendid choices including the two Harry's, Smitty's, Willy's, Ye Olde Chop House, Chateau Tavern, and Michael's 2. Also there are the true stalwarts of the district—traditional taverns with long and revered histories. Fraunces Tavern, reconstructed in the Georgian style of the original 1719 building, and once owned by Samuel Fraunces who later became President Washington's personal steward, even has its own museum above the restaurant. Ye Olde Dutch Tavern, located on the site of the John Street Theatre, has all the flavor of a mid-eighteenth-century bar-restaurant, and smaller establishments such as Emil's and the Brokers have a special character that comes from long and uninterrupted association with the area.

So readers should not dismiss downtown lightly. While it's true that the scene tends to be a little overmasculine during the day and that the clientele often lacks the variety found in uptown taverns, there is a growing vitality here, particularly in those places that remain open late into the night. Who knows, maybe the renaissance of downtown has just begun.

THE ATRIUM

ADDRESS: 100 Washington St. (at Rector St.); 344-3777
BAR HOURS: 11 A.M.–11 P.M. (1 A.M. on Fri.); closed Sat. and
    Sun.
FOOD: American and Italian (moderate)
CREDIT CARDS: AE BA CB DC MC and House Card
DRESS: Jacket and tie
SPECIAL FEATURES: Piano bar, cocktail hour with hot hors
    d'oeuvres 6 P.M.–8 P.M.
LIVELIEST TIMES: Most evenings, particularly Fri.

Giovanni Natalucci, once part-owner of the famed La Borsa restaurant on Pearl Street, recently opened this large establishment on the west side of downtown. Judging by its current popularity, it would appear that most of his admirers have moved with him. Even late in the evening, when many taverns in the area have closed their doors, both the bar and restaurant at the Atrium are going strong. Friday nights are particularly lively, and the older business crowd that dominates during the week is moderated somewhat by younger patrons from all over Manhattan and even Jersey.

Devotees of La Borsa will be relieved to know that Giovanni still maintains the high standard of his American and Italian cuisine. In addition to an excellent range of à la carte dishes (saltimbocca alla Romana, zuppa di pesce, chicken Scarpariello, veal Scaloppine), there's a "fully inclusive" dinner menu each night.

The dimly lit bar, pleasantly separated from the main dining area, attracts a real throng during the cocktail hour when there's piano music and a generous selection of hors d'oeuvres. However, if you'd like things a little more tranquil, come later.

BROKERS

ADDRESS: 46 Gold St. (between Fulton and John sts.); 962–0115
BAR HOURS: 9 A.M.–9 P.M.; closed Sat. and Sun.
FOOD: American (moderate)
CREDIT CARDS: AE BA CB DC MC and House Card
DRESS: Smart casual
SPECIAL FEATURES: Darts (tournaments on Mon., Tues, and Fri. evenings)
LIVELIEST TIMES: Usually 5 P.M.–8 P.M. Tues.–Fri.

A few decades ago, downtown was the wild, nightlife heart of the city, pumping with vigor and particularly conducive to the popular "pursuit of happiness." The Brokers tavern, located along a narrow section of Gold Street in a building erected as an inn in the 1870s, was part of the whole turbulent scene. During prohibition it was the notorious Van Axen's speakeasy. The first floor was a restaurant, the second a gin palace, the third and fourth a brothel—and the fifth a distillery. A truly integrated establishment!

Today, under the experienced ownership of Larry Rabin, Brokers is a slightly more restrained place although the regular darts tournaments, played on the two dart boards, attract a lively crowd of "Knickerbocker Leaguers" from uptown. Not only is this one of the few darting pubs downtown, but it boasts its own female team—The Broker's Aces—a welcome relief in the highly masculine environment of the area.

It's a pleasant, intimate place, not too easy to find but well worth the effort. The only problem is that, in common with the majority of downtown establishments, it closes far too early.

DOYLE'S CORNER PUB

ADDRESS: 70 Lafayette St. (at Franklin St.); WO 2–0353
BAR HOURS: 10 A.M.–midnight; closed Sat. and Sun.
FOOD: Irish/American and specials (moderate)
CREDIT CARDS: AE DC
DRESS: Casual
SPECIAL FEATURES: Cocktail hour 5 P.M.–7 P.M. (with hot and cold hors d'oeuvres on request)
LIVELIEST TIMES: 5 P.M.–10 P.M. Thurs. and Fri.

Ever felt like renting a pub for your own private party? Well, here's the place. For as little as $15.00 per person, Doyle's— complete with almost limitless food, drink, and entertainment (weekends only)—is yours for a few hours. It's the idea of Peggy Doyle, owner of one of the few relatively authentic Irish taverns in this part of Manhattan. Before taking over here a few years ago, Peggy and husband Sean owned the White Horse Inn—an upper east side establishment famous for its regular magazine, *The Horse's Mouth,* that featured poems and short stories by aspiring local writers. Unfortunately, a disastrous fire destroyed the place, so Peggy carried her boundless energy and enthusiasm downtown, where she exhibits that special knack for making patrons feel welcome, warm, and wanted. Even the most dour customer usually leaves with a grin or, occasionally, a new friend on his or her arm. The hardest people to make smile though, says manager Alfie McCourt, are the juries from the court buildings around Foley Square.

Because of its proximity to the courts, Doyle's inevitably attracts a regular clientele of judges and attorneys; yet there's little cliquish atmosphere. At lunchtimes, particularly, the crowd reflects the whole gamut of downtowners. Patrons are often lined two or three deep along the bar or around the tall marble-topped bar tables, waiting for a chance to sample the daily specials—stuffed flounder, linguini with clam sauce, shrimp marinara—or the regular Irish entrées of mixed grill, Irish sausages ("Bangers n' Mash"), and shepherd's pie. The porch café is a particularly popular place to dine and watch the passing street scene, although favored patrons often have meals delivered directly to their nearby offices.

Everyone seems to have such a good time at this pub. And that, according to Peggy, is as it should be. Her motto, "Why should the devil have all the good tunes" is most appropriate.

FRAUNCES TAVERN

ADDRESS: Pearl and Broad sts.; BO 9–0144
BAR HOURS: Noon–9 P.M. Mon.–Fri.; closed Sat. and Sun.
FOOD: American and European (expensive)
CREDIT CARDS: AE BA CB DC MC and House Card
DRESS: Smart
SPECIAL FEATURES: Upstairs museum
LIVELIEST TIMES: Variable

Rather than repeat the long and fascinating history of this renowned Manhattan landmark (which luckily escaped major damage in the 1975 Anglers Club bombing incident), we suggest you plan an extended visit there. There are brochures and pamphlets galore and a well laid-out museum on the upper floors where the story of Washington's farewell to his officers is told in every detail (it's still unclear whether the stoic-like general actually wept or was just rather embarrassed by the tender emotions of his colleagues).

Many tourists are surprised to find that a bar really exists here. But it's an attractive place in a club-like way, with deep leather wing chairs and a series of early American flags along the far wall (the barman has a pamphlet that describes the origins of each one). Somehow though, the canned music, acoustic-tile ceiling, and a most unfortunate vista across a car park seem a little out of place in this hallowed haven of history. (The restaurant, on the Broad Street side of the building, is pleasantly designed but expensive.)

HARRY'S AT THE
AMERICAN STOCK EXCHANGE

ADDRESS: 113 Greenwich St. (at Rector St.); 732–8736
BAR HOURS: 11 A.M.–11 P.M.; closed Sat. and Sun.
FOOD: American/European (expensive)
CREDIT CARDS: AE BA DC and House Card
DRESS: Jacket and tie
SPECIAL FEATURES: Decor and layout
LIVELIEST TIMES: Evenings late in the week

Harry Poulakakos (see HARRY'S AT HANOVER SQUARE) once raised bees in his native Greece. He was a most contented man and the future seemed tranquil and secure, until his father suggested he seek fame and fortune in the United States. Today Harry, his brother, and his wife, Edrienne, own two of the most successful establishments in downtown Manhattan; yet Harry still dreams of the day when he will return to his homeland and his bees.

This, his second restaurant, is a fascinating place located at the base of the American Stock Exchange. Prior to recent renovations it was a dull, institutional-type of bar-restaurant, often full of dull, institutional-type people. Today it's a little fantasy land—a replica of a narrow eighteenth-century street with adjacent, appropriately named dining rooms (the Patent Office, the Exchange Club, the Harbor Grill) and the delightful Back Office Bar. Each is distinct in character and decor, and each has its own following of regular patrons. The result could have been a little cutesy; but the whole concept has been carried off with flair and humor.

Edrienne Poulakakos, like husband Harry, is an unflappable manager, supported by a fine, experienced staff. The menu is almost identical to that at Hanover Square—except for the Friday special of bouillabaise à la Marseillaise, which seems to be one of the most popular dishes in the house.

Recent expansion of the Back Office Bar has made it a very pleasant haven for evening drinking (note the long hours) in a downtown place that's truly different.

HARRY'S AT HANOVER SQUARE

ADDRESS: 1 Hanover Square (between Pearl and Stone Sts.); 944–9254
BAR HOURS: 11:30 A.M.–1 A.M., closed Sat. and Sun.
FOOD: American/European (expensive)
CREDIT CARDS: AE BA CB DC MC and House Card
DRESS: Jacket and tie
SPECIAL FEATURES: Evening bar scene
LIVELIEST TIMES: Most evenings

A couple of years ago this was the famous Hanover Square Restaurant in the basement of India House—one of Manhattan's oldest landmarks housing one of Manhattan's most select clubs. Unfortunately the restaurant's fame, reputation, and cuisine had diminished and it was ripe for revamping. So along comes Harry Poulakakos bringing with him thirteen years experience at Oscar's Delmonico and a loyal and learned staff. Transformation! Even before Harry had time to hold his open-house party, the place

11

had regained and, in many ways, surpassed its predecessor's reputation. A larger bar was constructed and since that first day has never had a quiet lunchtime or cocktail hour. We were amazed by the number of well-dressed patrons who seemed quite content to be crammed, squeezed, and nudged into almost every niche and corner.

There's an almost Pavlovian rhythm at work in the Wall Street area. At the stroke of noon, the doors fly open and a steady stream of customers pours down the steps into the delightfully old-fashioned tavern and dining rooms. By 1:30 P.M. the stream reverses with equal intensity, and by 2 P.M. all that's left are a score of perspiring, slightly glassy-eyed waiters and Harry, cool as ever, directing mop-up operations and getting ready for the cocktail hour, when an ever-larger drinking crowd envelopes the place.

For all the apparent chaos, there's a remarkable sense of discipline and order here. Regulars are always greeted by name at the door, and by the time they reach the bar (a not altogether easy accomplishment) their drinks are sitting there, waiting for them. It's that kind of attitude that makes a good tavern.

Harry's cuisine, although expensive by uptown standards, is excellent—if you're lucky enough to get a table. At lunchtime, the attractive main dining room (dark panelled walls with murals of intoxicated monks!) is almost always full; and yet, the pace is relaxed and patrons feel unrushed.

Finally, note the bar hours. Harry's remains open long after most other downtown establishments have closed. Try to drop in one evening; but avoid the cocktail hour if you seek a little tranquility.

ROSIE O'GRADY'S SOUTH

ADDRESS: 211 Pearl St. (between Maiden Lane and John St.) 944–5174
BAR HOURS: 8 A.M.–4 A.M.; closed Sat. and Sun.
FOOD: American/Irish (moderate)
CREDIT CARDS: AE BA CB DC MC and House Card
DRESS: Smart casual
SPECIAL FEATURES: Live entertainment most evenings
LIVELIEST TIMES: 6 until closing Tues.–Fri.

It had to happen. A slice of the lively upper east side spirit has finally burst into the crusty, tradition-bound downtown scene. Austin Delaney and partner Mike Carty (manager of the other Rosie's at 41 Murray Street) thought it was time that downtown developed a night scene attractive both to businessmen in the area and the younger uptown and Jersey set. At Rosie's South they broke all the time-honored codes of the more respectable establishments in the area: They created a casual "pubby" atmosphere using rough beams, wooden slats, raffia matting ceilings, and AER Lingus posters; they introduced a less refined cuisine without elaborate sauces; they have a "party night" on Wednesdays with free drinks for the ladies between 6 P.M. and 7 P.M.; and they brought in high-quality entertainment—The Clancy Brothers, Tommy Makem, and Hal Roach.

13

While other taverns are closed and shuttered by 9 P.M., Rosie's blasts along until the early hours of the morning. Sometimes it's just too popular. One expects the familiar downtown lunchtime crush; but particularly on Friday nights, there are times when it's literally impossible to move from one end of the bar to the other.

Some disdainful tavern owners in the area are convinced Rosie's is merely a transitory fad. We doubt it. The scene is spreading, and new places like THE ATRIUM are opening up to the same lively, late-night crowd. Much as we love and respect the older places, the area needs new blood and a night scene. More power to Mike and Austin!

ST. CHARLIE'S

ADDRESS: 4 Albany St. (at Washington St.); 964–6940
BAR HOURS: 11:30 A.M.–11 P.M.; closed Sat. and Sun.
FOOD: American/European (moderate)
CREDIT CARDS: AE BA CB DC MC and House Card
DRESS: Smart casual
SPECIAL FEATURES: Live music—piano (Wed. and Thurs.);
    dixieland (Fri.); cocktail hour with hot hors d'oeuvres
LIVELIEST TIMES: We'll let you know in the revised edition

We intend to watch St. Charlie's very closely in the future. For all the effort that William Galvin and partner Betty Foley have put into its creation, it deserves to succeed.

Its western dockside location would at first not appear particularly conducive to strong evening trade. But there's something strange going on in this area. Four or five places have all opened recently and none have yet failed. One in particular, THE ATRIUM, is already a resounding success, and Galvin's other place just down the block, The Bull and Bear, has become a popular partying place, although the late-night scene is not too strong.

We love the flavor of St. Charlie's. It resembles a restrained Victorian café in one of those old, brooding hotels. There's a

huge grand piano by the door, large, curtained bow windows that face onto the street, a few strategically placed potted palms, and a series of delightful dining areas on different levels with subtle distinctions in decor.

The live music is varied and of a high standard (even the canned music features excellent jazz) and attracts a young, lively crowd. However, although lunchtimes are frantic, the night scene has not yet matured. But we'll keep hoping.

SKETCH PAD

ADDRESS: 91 South St. (at Fulton St.); 952–9645
BAR HOURS: 11:30 A.M.–2 A.M., closed Mon. (beer and wine only)
FOOD: Fresh seafood (inexpensive)
CREDIT CARDS: None
DRESS: Very casual
SPECIAL FEATURES: Live folk music occasionally; electric pianola
LIVELIEST TIMES: Varied and seasonal, but usually weekends

During one of those all-too-rare pauses in our search for hidden watering holes of downtown Manhattan, we popped into this tiny place opposite the South Street Seaport for a fish chowder. Not only was the chowder excellent and the taped chamber music most unusual; but the bar scene was one of the friendliest in the area. Our brief rest extended into an afternoon of conversation with many of the young ship renovators from the seaport. We learned much of the history of the area and even more about the traditions and tales of the soon-to-be-relocated Fulton Fish Market.

Summer is obviously the most popular time here. Tourists throng the wharves on warm weekends and even the regulars find it hard to get a seat at the Sketch Pad. However on evenings, earlier in the week, it's a little more tranquil. Owner Alex Fournier (a well-known portraitist) and George Peck, his manager, can spend more time chatting with customers, joking with old regulars like Ed Moran (an artist's dream of the ancient mariner), and enjoying the live folk music. It's a very gentle, open place.

There's just one problem. The Sketch Pad only offers beer and wine, so those who prefer the harder stuff are often given a couple of alternative locations by George. Just up the block near Pearl Street is the Square Rigger, an unadorned place that occasionally attracts the characterful patronage of old seafarers and captains. It's also become popular with a downtown lunchtime crowd who prefer a beer and a sandwich to some of the more elaborate offerings around the Wall Street area.

A second place is the Paris Bar, still part of the Meyers Hotel

(1873), at the corner of South Street and Peck Slip. Like the Square Rigger, it's a plain, predominantly masculine environ- ment, and has over 100 years of history and tradition behind it. But take a look at the magnificently ornate back bar, truly a masterpiece of its kind. It's a little dull during the day unless you happen to meet some of the hotel's seafaring residents (one couple has lived in the hotel for over fifty years). However, come in the very early morning when the fish market is in full swing and you'll get some of the real flavor of old Manhattan. It's worth getting up early and suffering the chill breeze off the East River to experience it.

17

SMITTY'S

ADDRESS: 5 Gold St. (between John St. and Maiden Lane); 943-2244
BAR HOURS: 11:30 A.M.–9 P.M. (11 P.M. on Fri.); closed Sat. and Sun.
FOOD: Seafood (moderate)
CREDIT CARDS: AE BA CB DC MC and House Card.
DRESS: Jacket and tie
SPECIAL FEATURES: Parties on public holidays
LIVELIEST TIMES: Fri. evenings

Smitty's has been a noted bar and seafood restaurant in this area since 1946 when Bob Smith first opened the place at 47 Fulton Street. In 1973 Bob's son Ira (who bears a remarkable resemblance to singer Tom Jones) and partner Neil Mosconi moved the establishment to its new Gold Street location—previously the site of another downtown landmark, Wolf's Delicatessen. Its reputation for finely prepared seafood has, if anything, improved since Ira took over. He's down at the nearby Fulton Fish Market early every morning selecting each day's supply and is resentful of the city's plan to relocate this noisy, bustling complex at Hunts Point in the Bronx. He also wonders what will become of such local culinary institutions as Sloppy Louie's and Sweets in the event of such a move.

Prior to becoming manager of the new establishment, Ira was chef for over nine years at his father's original place, so it's hardly surprising that the restaurant maintains a devoted following. The bar tends to be a little overcrowded at lunchtimes, a typical characteristic of downtown establishments. However, evenings are pleasantly relaxed except perhaps on Fridays when there's some live entertainment, and commuters come to celebrate the end of another week.

Decor is pleasantly varied: Rough wood floorboards contrast with an elaborate, rear-lit painted glass ceiling, and the wide, wedge-shaped bar area is relieved by cozy corner niches and booths. Downstairs is the major dining area, often used for private parties in the evenings. There's plenty of life in this rather "hidden" location.

WILLY'S

ADDRESS: 166 William St. (at Beekman St.); 962–9710
BAR HOURS: 11:30 A.M.–9 P.M.; closed Sat. and Sun.
FOOD: American and European (moderate)
CREDIT CARDS: AE DC MC and House Card
DRESS: Casual
SPECIAL FEATURES: Own bakery; cocktail hour 5 P.M.–8 P.M. with hot hors d'oeuvres
LIVELIEST TIMES: Evenings late in the week

Willy's has that special atmosphere of permanency, honesty, and good fellowship once characteristic of many of the old downtown tavern-restaurants. Unfortunately, in recent years such establishments have almost disappeared. The newer, fast-buck, gimmick-laden bars have taken their place and the concept of true "quality" has become synonymous with "old-fashioned." Mr. George Willy, we thank you for staying on and wish you continued success.

It's hard not to like this place. The waitresses in the first floor dining room, many of whom have been here for over twenty years, greet customers individually by their names and provide those little details of service that are the hallmark of a good restaurant. The place has its own bakery, well known for its dinner rolls, pies (including chicken and steak n' kidney) and an outstanding Black Forest cherry cake. At Christmas time mince pies are the true forte here, prepared with a homemade mince marinated for weeks in cognac.

As for the bar, that's downstairs to the left of the main entrance and, in the evening, provides a warm (if occasionally noisy) haven for wall-to-wall cocktail sippers. The restrained decor resembles a small *bierhaus* in Munich. Note the unusual ceiling and wall lamp shades which portray silhouetted reliefs of various artisan trades. These are still quite common in western Europe, but it's the first time we've seen them here. Also on the far wall (by a most unfortunately designed jukebox, the room's only discordant element) is a sketch of the street as it looked in the 1830s. Upstairs in the dining room is a fine series of murals including

19

one of a medieval feast on the rear wall (see if you can spot the unique example of artistic license).

The building itself is full of history. In 1839 it was a printing company and George Willy has retained the holes in the walls through which the machine belts used to pass, powered by a steam plant once located down the street. Little has changed here other than the replacement of the once-famous second floor cafeteria by a fine banquet room. Willy's is a truly authentic tavern and should not be missed.

YE OLDE CHOP HOUSE

ADDRESS: 111 Broadway (near Wall St.); 732–6166
BAR HOURS: 11:30 A.M.–7:30 P.M.; closed Sat. and Sun.
FOOD: American (expensive)
CREDIT CARDS: AE CB DC
DRESS: Jacket and tie
SPECIAL FEATURES: Location and ambience
LIVELIEST TIMES: Most evenings (but note early closing)

The menu cover claims that this is "the only cosy corner in the financial district." One patron we talked to however, described Ye Olde Chop House as an exclusive "non-dues-paying public club for the cream of Wall Street." In actuality, it's a little of each. The place certainly is cozy, snuggled in a subterranean setting off the subway entrance at the north end of the Trinity Church graveyard. The spacious bar area is separated by a partition from the rows of wooden booths that fill the dining area. It has an old bronze-colored masculine atmosphere. The walls are covered with a superb collection of sketches, lithographs, and photographs including a self-portrait by Caruso, two original Currier and Ives illustrations, and a rare sepia-colored photograph of Abraham Lincoln and his son.

The spirit of exclusivity comes not so much from the patrons who seem to reflect a cross section of downtowners, but more from the traditions of the place itself. Jackets and ties are essential; bar receipts, until recently, were cranked out on two ancient manual registers, and women rarely stand at the bar during the evening cocktail hour. Jac Kramer, third generation owner of the tavern, says that a few have tried it, but after five minutes of jostling, shoving, and elbow-jarring, have always returned to the tables.

Ye Olde Chop House has a history dating back to at least 1800 (a City Hall fire during that year destroyed many of the records pertaining to Manhattan's older buildings). Its original location was 118 Cedar Street. Jac Kramer's grandfather purchased Old Tom's as it was known in 1906; a shift was made in 1957 to 101 Cedar Street and later, in 1966, it was moved again to its present location.

21

In common with many downtown taverns, the lunch menu features a full range of entrees including a splendid selection of game and seafood dishes in season. Particularly notable are the venison steak, whole partridge, quail, mallard duck, soft shell crabs, and shad roe.

YE OLDE DUTCH TAVERN

ADDRESS: 15 John St. (between Broadway and Nassau St.); CO7-3532
BAR HOURS: 11 A.M.–9 P.M.; closed Sat. and Sun.
FOOD: German and American (expensive)
CREDIT CARDS: AE BA CB DC MC and House Card
DRESS: Smart informal
SPECIAL FEATURES: Atmosphere and history
LIVELIEST TIMES: Most evenings

The tavern's attractively modest appearance from the outside gives little indication of the riches within or its long and solid history. It can be appreciated on many levels. For the lawyers and stockbrokers who gather daily in groups by the long bar, it's a semiprivate club—a place to discuss mutual matters of interest and arrive at those crucial decisions so rarely recorded at official meetings. For connoisseurs of fine cuisine it offers a lengthy, but authentic, selection of American and German dishes (prepared according to one-time chef Franz Schilling's recipes) in addition to seafood and curry dishes for which the tavern is justly famous. Also, as a reminder of the old days, there's a splendid green turtle soup amontillado.

For lovers of history the tavern has much to offer. It was founded by Paul Langerfeld in 1900, when the neighborhood teemed with Amsterdam jewellers and Dutch craftsmen. At that time it was situated a little further down the street but was subsequently moved to its present location, once the site of the John Street Theatre (1767–1798) which in its pre-Revolution heyday

featured plays written and performed by Britishers for the delight of General Howe and his entourage. Later, George Washington is said to have sat, or slept, through occasional performances during his early residence in New York as president.

The tavern's more recent history, blurred slightly by prohibition and the operation of a speakeasy in the enclosed balcony above the main entrance, has been relatively tranquil; the place has matured like a fine cheese, ripe and robust. The last event of major significance was in 1974 when owner, Bob Timmins (Paul Langerfeld's son-in-law) protested the admission of women into this hallowed enclave of masculinity and fought his case through the courts—unsuccessfully. Ironically, though, the tavern has for many years featured a Shrove Tuesday pancake-eating contest, limited to females only, that invariably attracts considerable media attention.

The dark Dutch-styled wood fittings in the bar, throughout the long rear dining room, and around the balconies are all the work of Jacob Frolich, a once-famous tavern cabinetmaker. Also note the beer steins along the walls—without a doubt the finest collection in the city.

and for
your further enjoyment...

BARNABUS REX

155 Duane St. (off West Broadway); 962–9692

Here's one of the smallest and most unusual downtown taverns. The bar room, dominated by a large pool table, is a musty little enclave that attracts a bewildering assortment of local residents, actors, writers, and warehousemen, many of whose caricature portraits hang on the wall.

In the evening, the upstairs dining room is opened and occasional shows are presented—impromptu or otherwise. Unlike many taverns in the area it stays open late at night, and although it's an acquired taste, Barnabus Rex is invariably fun.

CHATEAU TAVERN

142 Pearl St. (at Wall St.); BO9–9768

Although known primarily for its fine cuisine, the Chateau attracts a lively drinking crowd to its Tudor-styled bar complete with side tables and booths. Upon entering the main door off Pearl Street (there's a second entrance off Water Street) patrons must first negotiate a forest of coatracks before emerging into the often turbulent confines of the bar counter (lunchtimes can often be a little too hectic). However, it's worth a visit. The drinks are excellent, there's usually an abundance of nibble-bowls, and it's a splendid place for eavesdropping if you're thinking of making changes in your portfolio.

EMIL'S

213 Pearl St. (between Maiden Lane and John St.); DI4–2348

Here's a lively place currently popular with the downtown insurance crowd that crams the place at lunchtime and returns in the evenings for a brief but generous presubway libation.

Since 1946 Emil's has been renowned for the quality of its cuisine. That was the year Emil Pangal left as manager of YE OLDE DUTCH TAVERN and took over here, much to the delight of his host of admirers. His menu and many of his recipes are still used today by Nick Karch, a former restaurant supplier who became owner in 1965. To keep his customers happy (downtown tavern owners are notoriously protective of their patrons) Nick has changed little in the old place. The tin ceiling, old photographs, and even the stag's head all remain. The intimate dining booths are the only recent addition and some of the older regulars even grumbled about that!

THE JOLLY MONK

59 Warren St. (at West Broadway); 233–9439

The name is most appropriate; it's always cheerful in this casual Irish tavern although, as with most places in the area, lunch times are frantic and the small tables are jammed with hamburger gluttons (10 ounces and good!) and Guinness drinkers.

The frontage is rather small—and invariably blocked by parked trucks—but you'll recognize the Jolly Monk by its window, plastered with signs advertising daily specials and staple dishes of shepherd's pie, London broil, and Irish stew. Inside, the decor is familiar: green derbies, shamrock signs, red-check tablecloths, ale barrels on the rafters, the inevitable dartboard, and always, always, lots of smiling faces.

MICHAEL'S 2

10 Hanover Square (at Pearl St.); 943–6767

Here's an unusually suave place on Pearl Street with a distinct gold and green decor, high-priced drinks, and a rather exclusive clientele. It doesn't appeal to every taste or pocketbook, but it's a fascinating way to observe the cream of Wall Street at play. Also, the sensitive layout and design of Michael's 2 provides yet another dimension to downtown drinking establishments.

MORGAN'S

134 Read St. (between Hudson and Greenwich sts.); 226–8928

This pleasantly refreshing place with a bright nautical flavor and a couple of fine "old New York" murals is located in an old building near the docks and attracts an interesting crowd of local businessmen and young residents from the Independence Plaza complex.

The waitresses, often dressed in long paisley skirts, are charming. The food is moderately priced and the atmosphere most relaxed. Also, there's an outside terrace for summer drinking and dining—most unusual for a downtown establishment.

EAST VILLAGE & SOHO

During the early 1600s, New Amsterdam's peg-legged governor, Peter Stuyvesant, decided he needed a farm. So, with minimal ceremony, he drove out the few remaining Indian squatters in the area from Broadway to the East River, bounded by what subsequently became Fifth and Seventeenth streets, and established a modest and prosperous estate. Later, around 1660, to improve access to his estate from his waterfront offices, he laid out a "wide and wondrous" avenue, the Bowery, appropriately befitting his status. In order to ensure some semblance of order in the landscape adjoining his avenue, he encouraged "free" slaves in the town to establish small holdings or "boweries" along part of its length. Typical of Stuyvesant's manner, this seemingly benevolent gesture had the effect of creating a barrier of dispensable citizens in case of Indian attacks.

Governor Stuyvesant died in 1672, but his town, renamed New York following the second British takeover in 1674, continued to prosper and expand northwards. Streets were laid out along the Bowery and during the early 1800s the area became home for thousands of poor immigrants.

In 1862, the Bowery Theatre was opened, heralding the Bowery's emergence as the entertainment center of a rapidly expanding and prosperous city. The Astor Opera House arrived in 1840 and for a while provided the cultural hub for wealthy residents around Astor Place and equally wealthy guests at the nearby Broadway hotels—the St. Nicholas, the Metropolitan, the New York, the American and Astor House. However, cultured society moved relentlessly northwards with the city, and the opera house lost much of its patronage, particularly following the 1849 riot against English actor William Macready who was accused of ignoring local talent in his productions. The fiery mob attempted to burn down the building, and in the skirmish 22 were killed and 150 wounded.

Tony Pastor understood the trends. He saw the scores of local theatres offering entertainment of a decidedly dubious nature, the gin mills, the grog shops, the "black and tan" beer dives, and the notorious "Bowery B'hoys" (immortalized by Charles Dickens in his *American Notes*). So rather than attempt to stem the wild tide of the Bowery spirit, he made vaudeville fashionable with his new Opera House, built in 1864.

What a street this was in the late 1800s! Beer halls flourished, catering to the local German population, often nicknamed "tangle-hairs" after that peculiar stupor brought on by excessive lager drinking. The magnificent Atlantic Garden combined the best of "beer hall" traditions with shooting galleries, orchestras, restaurants, and lunch counters, all enclosed by vast, elaborately frescoed arched ceilings. Even the popular lager palaces around Union Square could not compare with the Atlantic Garden or the even more elaborate German Winter-Gardens. They were imitated a score of times along the Bowery, but as journalist and social observer, James McCabe, Jr., discreetly explained at the time, "Not all of them are reputable. In some there is a species of theatrical performance which is often broadly indecent. The servant girl elements predominate in the audiences, and there is an unmistakably Irish stamp on most of the faces present."

The Bowery spirit boomed. Even in the Soho area, which by 1880 was emerging as a prosperous district of small factories housed in magnificent cast-iron structures, gin mills and "concert saloons" flourished. Down by the East River were the flophouses and dance houses catering to sailors and owned by such notorious gentlemen as John Allen, "the wickedest man in New York," who ran his brothels openly but proudly claimed that each room came equipped with a Bible! Not surprisingly, crime was rampant. The notorious murderer, Big Jack, even distributed printed fee schedules: "murder—up to $100; shot in arm—$50; slash on cheek—$10."

It was not until the great depression that the Bowery finally lost its spirit. Winos and bums littered the sidewalk. The great gardens closed. Few could afford the fleeting pleasure of the dance houses. The area sank into a long, slow decline. Even Union Square faded, and the beer halls folded leaving lonely Lüchow's as a last remnant of a once flourishing district.

There were, however, flickers of life in the 1950s and '60s. The East Village developed a unique, low-income bohemian character. The flower-power movement centered around the bars and taverns such as Stanley's (now Back East), Frogpond, and Kiwi II. Also in the last few years, off-Broadway theatre has found a new home on the Bowery. Phebe's, Tin Palace, The Colonnades, and Lady Astor's are all relatively new establishments catering to a thriving subculture clientele.

Most fascinating is the emergence of the Soho district as a center for artists, writers, and fringe groups who live in vast, high-ceilinged lofts and, within the space of a few brief years, have created one of the most culturally dynamic neighborhoods in Manhattan. The recent abandonment of the crosstown expressway proposal that would have annihilated some of the finest cast-iron buildings in the city and destroyed the neighborhood's subtle cohesion has given a new sense of purpose to its residents and new life to its pubs and taverns—Fanellis, Kenn's, Berry's, the Soho Darts Bar, and 162 Spring Street.

As for the old Bowery spirit, there's little left, except the undauntable McSorley's Ale House—a miniature monument to those wild times of the last century.

BACK EAST

ADDRESS: 196 Ave. B (at 12th St.); 228–3857
BAR HOURS: Noon–4 A.M.
FOOD: Sat. and Sun. brunch only, noon–4 P.M.
CREDIT CARDS: None
DRESS: Very casual
SPECIAL FEATURES: The urinals! Theatrical performances Fri., Sat., and Sun. 8 P.M.–10 P.M. ($2.50)
LIVELIEST TIMES: 8 P.M.–midnight Wed.–Sat.

There are few New York bars that can boast urinals dating back to the 1800s. In most places they seem to have been added as a casual afterthought, and the only thing they inspire is a hasty re-

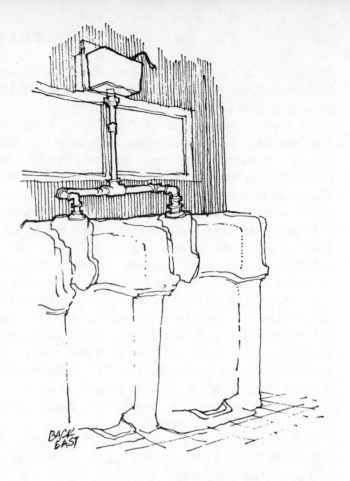

treat. But at Back East, customers often gaze in awe at the two great porcelain monoliths in the gentlemen's washroom.

The bar was originally established in 1892 by Peter Dolger, owner of the once-famous Dolger Brewing Company. In the early 1900s it was known as Stack's Bar, a neighborhood saloon for a predominantly German population. During the forties the Poles and Ukrainians moved in, and, according to Kevin Saviola, one of the bar's present owners, if you couldn't speak their native languages you had a hell of a time getting a drink.

A renaissance came in the sixties when Stanley Tolkin took over, renamed the bar Stanley's Place and made it the east side headquarters for the flower-power people—complete with art gallery and a beautifully renovated basement.

The demise of the flower movement coincided with Stanley's death in 1967, and the bar lost much of its appeal until the current owners took over in 1973 and began to revive it as a neighborhood meeting place.

Back East (the name reflects the gradual resurgence of the East Village) is now a delightfully authentic place, complete with carved back bar, stained glass panels, pendulum clocks, and those unique urinals. Artwork by local residents is displayed on the walls, and there's been a recent revival of the basement for impromptu theatrical performances ($2.00 donation).

The best time to visit is during the late evening when the bar does a great trade in Spaten München beer, served in tall Pilsner glasses with a slice of lemon. Alternatively, try the bagels, lox, and cocktail Sunday brunch; it's rapidly becoming a neighborhood tradition.

THE COLONNADES

ADDRESS: 432 Lafayette St. (at Astor Pl.); 473–8873
BAR HOURS: 3 P.M.–4 A.M.
FOOD: Varied (inexpensive)
CREDIT CARDS: None
DRESS: Very casual
SPECIAL FEATURES: Rear bocci court
LIVELIEST TIMES: 8 P.M.–2 A.M. Wed.–Sat.

The magnificent La Grange Terrace, otherwise known as Colonnade Row, is one of the finest remnants of old New York in this part of Manhattan. It was the work of artist, draftsman, and "architectural composer" Alexander Jackson Davis. Following its completion in the mid 1830s, it was regarded as one of the most sophisticated pieces of unified urban design in the city and home for many prominent families including the Astors and Vanderbilts. Even President John J. Tyler resided here for a while and was married on the second floor of one of the remaining town houses.

Until recently, owners of the structure have often failed to recognize its outstanding architectural qualities. In addition to demolishing five of the original nine townhouses, over the years there have been a score of incongruous additions including (al-

though fortunately not visible from the street) a complete five-story factory for the manufacture of Mother Sills Seasick Remedies!

For many years one of the basements was occupied by Conte's Italian Restaurant. However as the neighborhood declined, so did the quality of the food, and it only recently reemerged as The Colonnades bar under the enthusiastic management of Domenick Izzo and Bob Pauls. It's a fun place, full of local artists, film celebrities, writers, actors from the adjacent theaters, and students from nearby Cooper Union. It has its quieter periods, usually between 7 and 10 P.M. earlier in the week; but conversation and food (a limited but interesting menu) is always good. In fact many of the Colonnade's customers are regulars from the now abandoned Max's Kansas City, where Domenick was manager for a few years. If you liked that kind of crowd, you'll love it here.

The place has a number of notable features: magnificent door hinges from St. Patrick's Cathedral on Fifth Avenue, a colored engraving of the Eberhardt and Ober Brewing Company worth $1,500, a bocci court on the rear patio, and a host of magnificent cakes and pies by "Pamela."

FANELLI'S

ADDRESS: 94 Prince St. (at Mercer St.); 226–9412
BAR HOURS: 9 A.M.–midnight; closed Sun.
FOOD: American (inexpensive)
CREDIT CARDS: None
DRESS: Casual
SPECIAL FEATURES: Workingman's lunch
LIVELIEST TIMES: Most evenings

No study of Soho bars would be complete without mention of Fanelli's, a legend in the area and one of the oldest taverns—or cafés—in the city. It's here you can find both the old and the new Soho, especially at lunchtime when the modestly priced "workingman's" specials (roast beef, ravioli, corned beef, spare ribs, etc.) are served at tables covered with crisp white tablecloths to warehouse employees, businessmen, artists, writers, and all the miscellaneous members of humanity who make Soho such a fascinating and contrasting neighborhood.

Mike Fanelli, who is modestly reluctant to discuss his age or even the bar's fine reputation, can usually be found most days standing beside the massively ornate back-bar, alternately smiling and scowling at his diversified clientele. Most of the main wall is covered with photographs of old boxing champions—a reminder of the days when the bar was headquarters for the city's fight crowd—and the rear dining room remains virtually unchanged from that period.

On the outside, the flaking red paint, erratic neon sign, and steamy windows hardly suggest that this tiny place boasts of longevity and reputation envied by most other bars in the city.

35

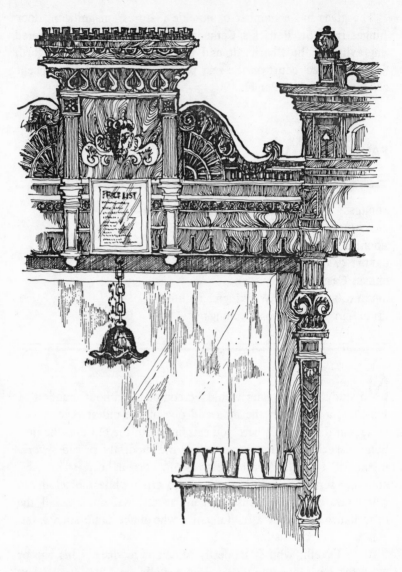

It's a no nonsense, no frills establishment. Many of the employees look as if they've been around since Soho was an attractive area of farms, and they've seen just about every kind of customer in New York.

The evenings are particularly enjoyable here. Conversation is excellent and it has that special flavor once thought unique to Left Bank bistros in Paris. If you want to get a feel of the real flavor, pop in on an early Saturday evening after the Soho galleries close.

KENN'S BROOME STREET BAR

ADDRESS: 363 West Broadway (at Broome St.) 925–2086
BAR HOURS: Noon–4 A.M.
FOOD: Hamburgers, salads, and pies (inexpensive)
CREDIT CARDS: None
DRESS: Very casual
SPECIAL FEATURES: Sat. and Sun. brunch noon–3 P.M.
LIVELIEST TIMES: Late evenings Wed.–Sat. and during brunch

Like most Soho bars, Kenn's is not an easy place to find. Look for a small pitched-roof building on the corner of West Broadway and Broome Street, its windows brimming with hanging plants, and the distinct aroma of broiling hamburgers wafting over a sidewalk occasionally cluttered with odd-looking pieces of rusted steel sculpture.

Although the bar has only been going for about two years under the management of Kenn Reisdorff, his wife, and his brother, it's become an integral part of the Soho scene—a meeting house for local artists and writers as well as an in place for upper east siders.

Originally this was a hotel on the northern fringe of the city. Then, as the surrounding farmlands gave way to urban expansion, it became a German restaurant in a predominantly German neighborhood (known to the residents as "Kleindeutschland" or "Little Germany"). For a while it was owned by the seven burly Wagner brothers, all Italians and all boxers. Even at that time, when 14th Street was considered uptown, it was a favorite place with New York's actors and artists—a reputation that has been recently revived as a result of Soho's transition from a somber warehousing and factory district to one of the most culturally dynamic communities in Manhattan.

Kenn and Soho have grown together. He lived here as an interior designer and "one step up from a cabinet maker" long before the neighborhood's renaissance, and he has put his talents to good use in his Broome Street establishment. The walls are a series of blackboards. Multicolored sticks of chalk are provided

37

for customers who feel the need to publicly express their wit and wisdom and contribute to New York's indigenous art form—graffiti. Above the bar (a combined effort of Kenn and his one-time partner, John) stands a huge stained-glass panel that Kenn extracted from his private storehouse of knickknacks and bric-a-brac. An even richer piece, once a window in a Philadelphia Society Hill mansion, forms part of the screen for the ladies' rest room.

The bar is many things to many people. Beer lovers rejoice in the Stegmaier Porter, Heineken, and McSorley's ale, all on tap. Gourmets relish the fine salads and outstanding Miss Grimble pies and desserts. Local residents scan the community notice board by the door in search of the ultimate loft or free kittens.

KIWI II

ADDRESS: 432 E. 9th St. (between Ave. A and First Ave.);
677–9990
BAR HOURS: Noon–4 A.M.
FOOD: Hamburgers, etc. (inexpensive)
CREDIT CARDS: None
DRESS: Very informal
SPECIAL FEATURES: The Krakatoa Cocktail; Sun. brunch starting
at noon
LIVELIEST TIMES: 9 P.M.–12 P.M. most evenings and during Sun.
brunch

K iwi II has to be seen to be believed. It's truly a neighborhood place (in a truly tough neighborhood), but it has a unique flavor. Speak with Jimmy Sampson (the last name is appropriate) and ask him to give you the fascinating tour of this tiny, rather musty bar. First he'll tell you about the speakeasy days when the bar windows were boarded up and patrons entered through an adjoining apartment doorway. Passwords, sliding mirrors, and steel bars on the door were all part of the routine. Next to the "Jean Harlow" ladies' rest room, notice the confessional. According to Jimmy, it's an old army type designed for instant erection in tight spots, which is not intended as a pun. But the rickety wooden structure does conceal "the honeymoon suite"—a single bed equipped with built-in-vibrator pads. Jimmy insists that it's for his personal use, so we'll leave it at that.

Stroll to the front of the place and take a look at the jukebox. In addition to a representative selection of current pop/folk features, there's an excellent collection of old jazz classics including Louis Armstrong's "Tin Roof Blues" and "Ain't Misbehavin'" by Fats Waller. Even at this point you've hardly started. Notice the collage wall of old prints, signed photos, scribbled notes, and pieces of poetry left behind by some of the bars more renowned patrons. By the side of the wall is a stack of crutches, for special use by "Krakatoa" victims. The name refers to a volcanic brew of 151 percent rum mixed with various fruit juices. It's misleadingly tasteful; however its potency is obvious from the list over the bar of unfortunates who entered the regular Krakatoa drinking contest and today shuffle around in a state of total abstinence, sad shadows of their former selves.

We could go on and on. Take a look at the menu, which sports Kiwi's motto, "Bad food, warm beer." It's a pretty apt summary of this unusual East Village bar.

McSORLEY'S OLD ALE HOUSE

ADDRESS: 15 E. 7th St. (near Third Ave.); 730–9044
BAR HOURS: 9 A.M.–1 A.M.; closed Sun.
FOOD: Specials and sandwiches (inexpensive)
CREDIT CARDS: None
DRESS: Informal
SPECIAL FEATURES: Tradition; McSorley's Ale on tap.
LIVELIEST TIMES: 9 P.M.–1 A.M. Fri. and Sat.

Tradition. In one word, that's McSorley's Old Ale House. And following the tradition set in 1854 by John McSorley, no women were allowed inside the pub until 1970, when it became law that there could be no sex discrimination in public establishments. But tradition was so strong that, when the bill was signed into law, Dorothy O'Connell Kerwin, whose father bought the tavern in 1937, would not break the tradition and be the first woman to enter. And to the day she died Mrs. Kerwin never set foot in the tavern during operating hours.

This is the kind of place where anyone can get a glass of ale (and only ale is sold), talk with friends, and reflect on old times. McSorley's invites reminiscenses. The sawdust-covered floors, battered wooden tables, memento-laden walls, and potbellied stove are as they always have been—a bit musty, historic, and unpretentious. Workshirts, worn flannel jackets, that comfortable old hat are all de rigueur here.

The world outside has changed, but other than the occasional female patrons, McSorley's has stayed just the same. Bartender John Smith has been here for thirty-three years; a letter of ac-

40

knowledgment presented to John on his thirtieth anniversary and signed by many of McSorley's famous patrons, hangs on the wall along with other accumulated photographs and memorabilia.

There is no music, and the television set is turned on only for major sporting events and national happenings. It is a meeting place for people who wouldn't usually meet: Lawyers, theatre people, cab drivers, university professors, and students might all be crammed together at a table while quenching their thirst with McSorley's own ale. The walls testify to the fact that Brendan Behan and others used to carouse here (Brendan's chair is in the far left corner of the front room). In fact the notable Irish playwright gave a loving description of the place in his book *Brendan Behan's New York*. A lot of history has passed through McSorley's.

ORCHIDIA RESTAURANT

ADDRESS: 145 Second Ave. (at 9th St.); 730–9479
BAR HOURS: Mon.–Thurs. 4 P.M.–2 A.M.; Fri.–Sun. noon–3 A.M
FOOD: Italian and East European (moderate)
CREDIT CARDS: None
DRESS: Very casual
SPECIAL FEATURES: Spaten München beer
LIVELIEST TIMES: 8 P.M.–midnight Fri. and Sat.

A neighborhood often changes because its residents move on to other, scattered neighborhoods. But if the people leave behind a part of their culture, they'll come back to their old stomping grounds to visit what remains and to congregate once more.

One of the best examples of this cultural tradition is to be seen at the Orchidia Restaurant in the East Village. The area used to be part of the old "Gashouse" district and children of Ukrainian families who once lived here, gather together to compare notes and discuss changing times. These are young men and women, mainly college students, who return to the Orchidia to drink the Spaten München beer (with a slice of lemon) and eat pizza and flanken. The owner, Mrs. Pidhorodecky, takes a motherly interest in them and tries to make sure no student starves (and, with her ebullient cuisine, that's not too hard). Of course there are many other customers attracted to the Orchidia by its warmth and relaxed atmosphere.

The bar is small and only seats about five people, but no one is pressured to eat at the tables. Since the neighborhood has so few inviting watering holes, many of the people currently living, working, or studying in the area stop by, particularly on Friday nights when the small, dark, one-room restaurant-bar is packed with patrons from the nearby N.Y.U. School of the Arts, the Negro Ensemble Company, or the neighborhood generally. It's a delightfully different kind of establishment with a set of traditions all its own.

PHEBE'S

ADDRESS: 361 Bowery (at 4th St.); 473-9008
BAR HOURS: 5 P.M.–4 A.M.
FOOD: American (moderate)
CREDIT CARDS: AE BA CB DC MC
DRESS: Casual
SPECIAL FEATURES: Theatre atmosphere
LIVELIEST TIMES: 10 P.M.–2 A.M. Wed.–Sun.

The whitewashed walls of Phebe's stand out like white linen hung on a clothesline with dirty, old rags. While most of the other buildings on the Bowery are encrusted with the ages, Phebe's is challenging the Bowery's reputation as a neighborhood of "last resort." And it's succeeding.

Phebe's owner, Lester Nichols, thinks the Bowery is a fine place and is convinced that it's on its way back up again. The dining and drinking crowd here comes from what Mr. Nichols considers the area's main cohesive, expanding industry: the theatre. Earl Wilson has even referred to Phebe's as the "Sardi's of Off-Broadway." Let's make that off-off Broadway too.

Mr. Nichols has put a lot of love and labor into earning the appreciation and respect of this local theatre crowd. The long dining and drinking area in the room adjacent to the bar is lit by mini-spotlights focused on the show posters hung along one long wall. Red carpeting and wooden booths add to the dimly lit "after-theatre" atmosphere.

But remember, this is after-theatre, off-Broadway, off-off-Broadway, and off-experimental Broadway. People who stop by for a drink have probably just come from the La Mama or the Truck and Warehouse theatres, and are going to be dressed casually. However, since Phebe's has been discovered by the theatre crowd, many luminaries make a special trip from the Great White Way itself for Phebe's fine drinks, hamburgers, and one-pound boneless steaks.

The "madness" at Phebe's, as Mr. Nichols calls it, starts between 9 P.M. and 10 P.M. Wednesday through Sunday—the operating days of the local theatres. Then it's elbow-to-elbow conversation about what's happening locally. And apparently, many people feel that what's happening is happening at Phebe's.

SOHO DARTS BAR

ADDRESS: 60 Mercer St. (at Broome St.); 966–3382
BAR HOURS: Noon–4 A.M.
FOOD: American and European (inexpensive)
CREDIT CARDS: None
DRESS: Casual
SPECIAL FEATURES: Darts, live music, cellar cabaret
LIVELIEST TIMES: 8 P.M.–4 A.M. Tues. and weekends

Here's another recent addition to the burgeoning bar scene in Soho. Take an old nuts and bolts factory complete with vast cellar, a mini-mezzanine in Victorian gothic style, and a twenty-five foot high ceiling. Add a long homemade bar consisting of beer barrels and scraps of plywood. Clean the old brick walls, scatter a few tables, chairs, and posters around and place two competition dart boards in strategic locations, and you've created an ideal local pub for the artists, writers, and other residents of this fascinating Manhattan neighborhood.

That's exactly what Nicky Virachkul, a former javelin thrower from Thailand, and Bob Bonic, one-time NYU professor of mathematics, have done; and it works beautifully! Within a few short months this place has become the new mecca of darts throwers from all over the metropolitan area. Part of the attraction of course is Nicky, who in addition to being champion of New York's "Knickerbocker darts league" also placed second in the 1975 U.S. Open, losing narrowly to the renowned Conrad Daniels.

Tuesday night is tournament night here so if you've ever wondered what the current darts craze is all about, come and watch some of the local teams: Cannon's Uglies (Cannon's bar); Glocca Grande (GLOCCA MORRA); The Waltzing Wallabies (WALTZING MATILDA); Jacque's Transplants (VILLAGE CORNER); Felle's Pineapples (FELLE'S TAVERN), etc.

If you'd like an impromptu lesson, come on one of the quieter weeknights and challenge Nicky to a game of 301. If he's in top form it won't last long; but at least you'll have been beaten by one of the best in the country.

45

The place is still expanding and changing. Nicky and Bob hope to open the cellar as a night spot for music and theatre, and although the menu is mainly American, their Russian chef occasionally excels herself with some outstanding and unusual specials.

It's truly a great pub and well worth a special trip—if only for the draft Bass ale, one of England's finest exports.

TIN PALACE

ADDRESS: 325 Bowery (at 2nd St.); 674–0566
BAR HOURS: 3 P.M.–4 A.M. Mon.–Sat.; noon–4 A.M. Sun.
FOOD: Hamburgers, etc. (inexpensive)
CREDIT CARDS: None
DRESS: Very casual
SPECIAL FEATURES: Live jazz; Sun. brunch noon–5 P.M.
LIVELIEST TIMES: 10 P.M.–2 A.M. Thurs.–Sun.

The colorful history of the Bowery includes a tradition of grass roots jazz. However the street's decline following the depression rapidly curtailed such traditions and it's only within the last two or three years that a resurgence has begun, thanks to places like Tin Palace, PHEBE'S, THE COLONNADES, and LADY ASTOR'S. While the house group at the Tin Palace plays Brazilian-oriented jazz, many big names like Ron Carter, Howard Johnson, and Jimmy Giuffre have sat in with the Lloyd McNiell Quartet.

But jazz isn't the only thing the Tin Palace has to offer. Paul Pines and his partner, Michael Spirer, have created a spot where all types of people—from blue-collar workers to those in the arts—can meet, mix, and drink in a place with true neighborhood spirit. Mr. Pines has worked in East Village and Soho bars for a long time. He saw the Bowery undergoing a slow rebuilding process during the past few years and felt that it could once again be the hub of a thriving locality. In fact, he thinks of the Bowery as frontier living, where things must be started from scratch and where faith in the area plays an important part in success.

So far, his faith has been rewarded. After six months of renovating what used to be a typical Bowery wino bar, he and his partner opened to a crowd of old friends. Now, through word of mouth, they have expanded, adding outdoor cafés on two sides of the tavern. The back-bar is the same one that has always been there, only it has been stripped and refinished to reveal its unusual art deco character. A carved wood railing from the old Broadway Central Hotel (which recently collapsed) separates the serious drinking zone from the tables and chairs. On Friday and Saturday there's a $2.00 per person cover charge to hear the jazz, but if you stand at the bar, there's no minimum and you can nurse a beer a long time. (Once you sit on the other side of the railing, however, there is a minimum of $2.50 per person.) No problem. Since Mr. Pines caters to what he calls "experimental eaters," you can always spend the minimum on such delights as fresh spinach pie, crêpes, hot buttered rum, or café royal.

and for
your further enjoyment...

BERRY'S

180 Spring St. (between West Broadway and Thompson St.);
226-4394

Only recently, Kenn Reisdorff and his wife, Berry (owners of
KENN'S BROOME STREET BAR) opened a small bar-restaurant,
Berry's, on nearby Spring Street. The decor here is a masterpiece
of restrained Victoriana, and the place features Watney's and
Dinkel Acker on tap. Although it's too early to tell for sure, the
beaming faces of the customers, both at the bar and the small
dining tables, suggest that Kenn and Berry have provided yet
another successful addition to Soho's social attractions.

THE FROGPOND

414 E. 9th St. (between First Ave. and Ave. A); 473–9483

Close to KIWI II is another funky East Village spot with a wild and checkered history. Owner Hiader Beqaj is particularly proud of the bullet hole in the ceiling! Actually, the neighborhood has mellowed a little since the fifties when it was known for its street gangs à la *West Side Story*; today the Frogpond caters to an integrated, and usually mild-mannered, clientele. Notice the magnificent mural—a mirror reflection of the bar with patrons painted as frogs. It's a crazy place—somewhat of an acquired taste—but well worth a visit.

LADY ASTOR'S

430 Lafayette St. (at Astor Pl.); 228–7888

While Domenick Izzo and Bob Pauls (owners of THE COLONNADES) deserve much credit for maintaining life and character in the magnificent Colonnades landmark building, even more laurels must be bestowed upon Robert Ogden who, with his adjacent Lady Astor restaurant and tavern, has created one of the finest refurbished establishments in the city. We will say no more because the quality and mood of the place speak volumes, and management is apprehensive of excessive publicity. We merely offer a humble thank you to Mr. Ogden and his many friends who have performed a great service by preserving and enhancing one of the last great architectural masterpieces in this area.

LÜCHOW'S

110 E. 14th. St. (at Irving Pl.); GR 7–4860

Lüchow's is a place that must be seen—a symbol of old New York elegance that remains a magnificent retreat from today's plastic world (even though it happens to be owned by one of the largest restaurant companys in the country). For ninety-three years Lüchow's has served a crowd ranging from renowned celebrities to the mixed-bag residents of changing 14th Street. Its appeal is easy to understand. The interior is reminiscent of an enormous dining room on a classic trans-Atlantic liner. Dark woods dominate and nostalgia fills the air. It used to be one of the favorite places of Lillian Russell and Diamond Jim Brady, and now there are banquet rooms named in their honor, the one bearing Miss Russell's name complete with a cabinet of valuable memorabilia.

51

Upstairs, an area rarely frequently by Lüchow's regulars, is the delightful Steinway Room named in honor of William Steinway, the master of piano makers. Steinway Hall used to be located directly opposite Lüchow's, and it was with the financial backing of the Steinway family that August Guido Lüchow was able to open his humble establishment in 1872. Lüchow, a gentleman of remarkable character and capacity, not only made this the best-loved beer hall in the Union Square area (once renowned for its Bavarian flavor), but also became known for his ability to gulp down twelve pints of Würzbürger beer from a huge porcelain tankard in a single short sitting.

The popularity of Lüchow's German cuisine has overshadowed its reputation as a drinking spot. However, there's a splendid bar here with an active lunchtime scene and it's well worth a visit.

162 SPRING STREET

162 Spring St. (at West Broadway); 431–7637

The owners of this bar-restaurant are wary of excessive publicity because they want to preserve the place as it is now—an integral part of the Soho neighborhood. However, it's a very inviting spot, somewhere you can go for a relaxed drink and conversation as long as you sit at the bar or on the raised seating area nearby. It also has a very distinctive design—a sort of Corbusier environment—and almost everything, including various pipes and fixtures, is painted brown with an occasional gold stripe running along the walls and down the bar. It was opened originally because there was no place to eat or drink in the area, and the owners felt that such a great neighborhood needed somewhere for the local artists and writers to meet. That's still its prime function, but if people from outside the neighborhood don't come on like tourists, they can mingle and enjoy the mood of Soho so subtly nurtured here.

GREENWICH VILLAGE

The Village remains one of Manhattan's most remarkably homogeneous neighborhoods. While its pubs and taverns reflect a wide spectrum of history, interests, and pursuits, the physical character of the area with its narrow brownstone streets and quiet residential courts provides a unity of environment unmatched in Manhattan. Doubtless Sir Peter Warren, a British Naval officer and possible gentleman pirate, would still recognize parts of his Greenwich Estate which was subdivided and developed spasmodically in small tracts after 1730. The disjointed street pattern would appear most appropriate to an Englishman whose homeland cities grew along meandering market-bound cart tracks.

Throughout the last three and one-half centuries the Village has always been regarded as an area of refuge. One of the first Dutch governors of New Amsterdam, Wouter Van Twiller, used to rest from his official labors by growing tobacco in his "Bossen Bouwerie" (farm in the woods) near the Hudson. During the regular smallpox and yellow fever epidemics that plagued the downtown community in 1739, 1797, and 1822, Greenwich Village developed as a flourishing community, famous for the quality of its air and water. Even the customs house, the post office, and many banks (hence Bank Street) relocated to this desirable suburb. In the early nineteenth century Washington Square, previously a Potters Field burial ground, place of public execution, and parade ground (in that order) became a fashionable park, residential area, and home of New York University.

By the early 1900s, however, parts of the Village had entered a period of decline. Tenements were erected and noxious industries lined the streets around the crowded Hudson wharves. The elite, ever wary of New York's northward growth, began to move out as the less fortunate Irish, European, and Chinese immigrants created teeming slums in Little Italy, Chinatown, and the southern fringes of Greenwich Village.

Attracted by the low rents and the casual life-style of the area, other groups began to find the Village a delightful refuge. During the early 1900s writers, artists, and intellectuals, loosely categorized by their critics as bohemians, moved into small apartments and lofts along the narrow, tree-lined streets. Edgar Allan Poe, who wrote his "Gordon Pym" and "Fall of the House of Usher" in the 1840s at his 3rd Street home, was regarded by many as the pioneer of this movement, and he was followed in turn by such notables as Walt Whitman, Mark Twain, Bret Harte, Edith Wharton, and Henry James. However, the bohemian spirit included the vociferous fringe elements, such as Piet Vlag, founder of *The Masses* journal, and Upton Sinclair, whose liberal club on MacDougal Street featured wild orgies known as "Pagan Routs" above anarchist Polly Hollyday's restaurant on the ground floor. In 1915 the club also became the home of the Washington Square Players—the first group to feature Eugene O'Neill's controversial productions.

After World War I the bohemian crowd of angry young men degenerated somewhat as the Village once again offered an ideal refuge for true eccentrics, most notable of whom was Christine Elle, a baroness who sported a vermilion-painted, shaved head and invariably walked the street with a pet leopard on a leash.

The cultural decline continued during and after World War II when the Village developed distinct honky-tonk and Times Square characteristics which, in the opinion of many observers, have only recently disappeared.

However, during the fifties there was a new influx of artists and intellectuals. Again, another label was used to categorize such individuals, that of "beatnik"—a sort of updated bohemian. But the trend continued and in the sixties brought the hippies and the flower-power movement. Folk and jazz clubs were all the rage. The murkier the cellar the more popular was the place. Amazingly, many, such as the Village Vanguard, Folk City, the Other End, the Bottom Line and the Bitter End, have shown remarkable endurance, although they are beginning to be overshadowed by some of the newer jazz pubs such as Sweet Basil, Bradley's, Jacque's, and St. James' Infirmary.

The literary and art scene, although somewhat dissipated by

the emergence of Soho and the new Village on the upper west side, still continues to support such traditional taverns as Chumley's, the Lion's Head, the White Horse Tavern, Broadway Charly's, the Cedar Tavern (once the hub of the Jackson Pollock/Willem de Kooning Tenth Street School) and to a lesser extent, Benchley's Pub and the Sazerac House in the West Village, both frequented by residents of the Westbeth artists' complex.

Most notable, however, in the last few years has been the emergence of the Village gay community and a reestablishment of the neighborhood café society. In the former instance, a large number of taverns have opened recently, catering almost exclusively to this group (and unfortunately it is this exclusivity which precludes them from review in this book). In the latter case, there are many taverns that provide congenial café flavor, including Gottlieb's, Jimmy Day's (in the summer), Sweet Basil, Buffalo Road House, the Locale, Adam n' Eve, and William Shakespeare's.

The Village continues to change. In some instances it has become a little "cutesy," and a few of the once-respected taverns, particularly those along the major avenues, have overpandered to commercial tastes. Nevertheless, the old spirit is still alive and well and living along those narrow streets hidden behind the overfashionable storefronts.

BENCHLEY'S PUB

ADDRESS: 611 Hudson St. (at 12th St.); 989–7370
BAR HOURS: Noon–1 A.M.
FOOD: American and specials (moderate)
CREDIT CARDS: AE DC MC
DRESS: Casual
SPECIAL FEATURES: Nautical decor, Sat. and Sun. brunch
LIVELIEST TIMES: 7 P.M.–10 P.M. Thurs.–Sun.

The porch-café suggests that Benchley's is quite a sizeable establishment. In fact, it's really a small, intimate room brimming with nautical knickknacks: figureheads, old lithographs, maps,

55

paintings, and even ashtrays from early twentieth-century steamers. In a framed case by the rest rooms is a key to the pilothouse of one of the many Great Lakes liners designed by the grandfather of current owner Jack Herbert. The building itself was also the home of a sea captain during the mid-1800s when this was part of the rough and tumble dockside area and the adjoining structure housed an elaborate "place of ill-repute." In later years, it was a butcher's shop until the fortunate owner won a bonanza in the state lottery and retired to a glorious paradise.

Like many of the pubs in the West Village, Benchley's attracts a crowd of local regulars including many of the artists from nearby Westbeth—that notable experiment in creative community living housed within the remodelled Bell Telephone Laboratories.

In addition to the bar, which features Prior's dark on tap, Benchley's is well known for its sturdy American cuisine. The ⅓-pound lunchtime "steerburgers" (eight varieties including an excellent baconburger) are particularly popular, although there are more elaborate dishes in the evening including Alaska king crab legs, chicken and beef teriyaki, striped bass almondine, fish 'n' chips, and broiled sirloin au gratin. If you're stuck for a choice, there's a splendid and inexpensive chili served with French bread.

THE BLEECKER STREET

ADDRESS: 302 Bleecker St. (at Seventh Ave. S.) ; YU 9–3907
BAR HOURS: Noon–4 A.M.
FOOD: Varied (inexpensive)
CREDIT CARDS: None
DRESS: Casual
SPECIAL FEATURES: Sat. and Sun. brunch
LIVELIEST TIMES: Varies, but usually 6 P.M.–11 P.M.

The first time we visited this Village locale, goldfish were flapping around the fountain pool in the garden patio, Sam Catt (the resident feline) was sprawled beneath an ancient Silvertone gramophone on which a 78 rpm record revolved sluggishly, and Phil di Biaso, the owner, was huddled with a group of friends by the bar looking for all the world like just another customer.

He's a modest, self-effacing man, proud of his bar's spirit of cama-raderie and the fact that many of the resident celebrities in the area can spend an evening at the Bleecker Street without hassle. His only regret is that some New York newspaper journalists regard this place so much as their own personal watering hole that they never mention it in their copy for fear of attracting at-tention to the bars relaxed, low-key atmosphere.

Decor is basic: brick walls, occasionally doubling as a gallery for local artists, worn wooden tables, a few Tiffany-type lamps (and a genuine one) and, at the time of our visit, a small ter-rarium by the door that Phil had recently completed. Perhaps most attractive, especially on a warm summer night or during the weekend brunch session (a great bargain, 1 P.M.–5 P.M. Sat. and Sun.) is the rear patio—a small, enclosed space with ivy-colored walls overlooked by some of the Village's oldest buildings. It's a little world unto itself, a great place to unwind or dine on the bar's reasonably priced dishes.

BRADLEY'S

ADDRESS: 70 University Pl. (between 10th and 11th sts.); 228–6440
BAR HOURS: Noon–4 A.M.; 5 P.M.–3 A.M. Sat. and Sun.
FOOD: American and continental (moderate)
CREDIT CARDS: AE
DRESS: Casual
SPECIAL FEATURES: Live jazz nightly 9:30 P.M.–2 A.M.
  ($3.50 minimum at tables during music)
LIVELIEST TIMES: 9 P.M.–2 A.M. Thurs.–Sat.

In its five short years of existence, Bradley's has become a Vil-lage legend, popular both with jazz lovers and professional mu-sicians who regard the tavern as a true bastion of good modern jazz. Of course the owner, Bradley Cunningham, is something of a legend himself. He's tended bar in places all over the Village, owns one of Manhattan's last "hole-in-the-wall" bars ('55') and counts among his friends some of the best-known names in modern jazz. Zoot Simms, Stan Getz, and Joe Beck have all made impromptu appearances here, and billings recently included Al Haig, Percy Heath (MJQ), Jimmy Raney, and Jimmy Rowles.

The crowd is a typical Village mixture, and not everyone comes just for the music. The dining room boasts a short but interesting dinner menu that includes duck orientale, sole almondine, stuffed trout, and braised sweetbreads served against a pleasant decor of low lights, lithographs, original oils, and dark wood-panelled walls. The atmosphere is relaxed and slightly conservative—unless of course you visit on a weekend evening when the place is packed.

If you prefer a more subdued ambience in which to appreciate Bradley's fine music, come on any night, Sunday through Wednesday. If you stay late enough, you might even catch a glimpse of Bradley himself at the piano.

CEDAR TAVERN

ADDRESS: 82 University Pl. (between 11th and 12th sts.), 675–9555
BAR HOURS: 10 A.M.–4 A.M.
FOOD: American (moderate)
CREDIT CARDS: None
DRESS: Casual
SPECIAL FEATURES: Clambake, Sat. and Sun. brunch noon–4:30 P.M.
LIVELIEST TIMES: Most evenings from 9 P.M.

Sandwiched between two stately but overbearing buildings on University Place is the (relocated) Cedar Tavern—once the center for the Jackson Pollock/Willem de Kooning "Tenth Street School" society. Much has changed, however, since those days in the fifties when "going down to Tenth Street" with its avant-garde galleries was a regular pilgrimage for those considering themselves connoisseurs of contemporary art. Now Soho with its lofts and high white galleries is the new nucleus for the "isms"

of art. Yet the Tavern, with a newly constructed greenhouse on
its roof (complete with bird calls and running waterfalls), lives
on and offers a delightful choice of moods.

Downstairs the room is dominated by a massive wooden bar
over 100 years old and originally from the old Susquehanna
Hotel (it was 20 feet longer at that time). Local secretaries, bank-
ers, and publishers, stop by here for an afternoon break. Celebrities like Al Pacino drink here, and while they may be recognized, they won't be hassled.

59

Upstairs is the "garden" under a 60-foot glass roof: The bar is a drinking well, the tables are either World War II ship hatch covers or giant slices from Guatemalan fruitwood trees; plants abound, sunshine or starlight spills through the roof, and the mood is relaxed.

For drinking, try the hard-to-find beers available here: Würzbürger and Prior on tap. For dining, there's prime ribs on a spit, daily specials, a Saturday and Sunday brunch, and the Tavern's specialty—its famous clambake. While there is an occasional poetry reading, and the owners are considering allowing improvisational theatre performances upstairs, entertainment is not the key here. At the Cedar Tavern, you'll find interesting people and interesting times.

CHUMLEY'S

ADDRESS: 86 Bedford St. (at Barrow St.); 989–9038
BAR HOURS: 5 P.M.–2 or 3 A.M.; opens at noon Sat. and Sun.
FOOD: American/Indonesian (moderate)
CREDIT CARDS: None
DRESS: Very casual
SPECIAL FEATURES: Poetry reading 2 P.M. Sat.; Sun. brunch noon–4 P.M.
LIVELIEST TIMES: 8 P.M.–2 A.M. Thurs.–Sat.

If John Steinbeck or Ring Lardner were to revisit some of their old New York hangouts and stopped by Chumley's, they would probably recognize it immediately. Very little has changed since they used to gather with James Joyce, John Dos Passos, and the tavern's owner, Lee Chumley, to discuss their current literary endeavors. It is even rumored that Joyce wrote several chapters of *Ulysses* at a corner table here. Dust jackets from many books written during that period are exhibited today, as they were then, when they were used to promote new works.

Former devotees also recognize the original unmarked entrance—unmarked because the tavern began as a speakeasy. There still aren't any signs, and the regular clientele feel as if they are

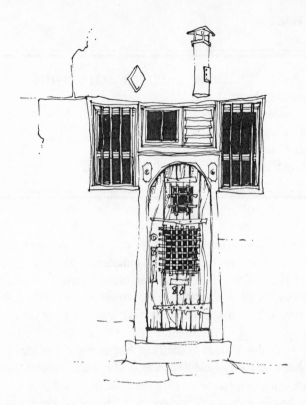

entering a private and very personalized club with the aura of an early Bogart movie. For those in the know, there's also another entrance complete with buzzer through a back courtyard, left over from the speakeasy era.

Because Chumley's is so "hidden" (even we've had problems locating it on return visits) most of the patrons don't just drop in. They know exactly where they're going, and some regulars make the trek from as far afield as New Jersey and Long Island.

An evening at Chumley's invites long conversation across old initial-carved tables over good drinks and food. Complete dinner service stops about 11:30 P.M., after which late-night suppers are served to crowds often from the local universities. So if food is a primary concern, come a little earlier and try Chumley's special Indonesian rice or the fresh seafood for which the restaurant is so justly famous. Or, if you're in the Village on a Saturday afternoon at 2 P.M., have a beer and enjoy the weekly poetry reading. Remember, though, that Chumley's only seats about seventy-five people, and if the poet is popular, the seats will be too.

61

GOTTLIEB'S

ADRESS: 343 Bleecker St. (at W. 10th St.); 929–7800
BAR HOURS: Noon–1 A.M.
FOOD: American/Italian/Oriental (inexpensive)
CREDIT CARDS: AE BA MC
DRESS: Casual
LIVELIEST TIMES: Weekends 10 P.M.–2 A.M.

Bill Gottlieb (described by some of his friends as an "up-and-coming real estate tycoon and sometimes playboy") recently opened this delightful little bar-restaurant following the outstanding successes of his two other Manhattan establishments—the Casserole (Hudson and Perry streets) and the Inca (at the western extremity of 12th Street). It's still in the process of synthesis with the Village scene, but has already developed a distinct late-night theatrical following. The walls around the small bar area are covered with theatrical posters, although the space above the fireplace is usually reserved for one of Leonardo Velasco's overpowering portraits. At the time of our visit, we sat at one of the bar's marble tables and were regarded with enormous disdain by Velasco's rendering of a fat prima donna wrapped in red ostrich feathers.

Reluctantly, Bill removed most of the fine stained-glass windows, again the work of Velasco, in order to give passersby a glimpse of the bar's intimate interior and a view of the restaurant patrons devouring some of Gottlieb's unusual dishes—a fine risotto served with saffron rice in a "casuela," the amazing Gottlieb salad with its ten ingredients, and such unfamiliar appetizers as chomos, clams à la España, and Thai fish balls.

Busiest nights tend to be on the weekend, so if you're looking for a quieter atmosphere, try Gottlieb's any evening Monday through Thursday.

HORN OF PLENTY

ADDRESS: 91 Charles St. (at Bleecker St.); 242–0636
BAR HOURS: 4:30 P.M.–2 A.M.
FOOD: A fascinating variety (moderate)
CREDIT CARDS: AE BA CB DC MC
DRESS: Casual
SPECIAL FEATURES: Outdoor dining patio
LIVELIEST TIMES: Mid-evenings, particularly weekends

Horn of Plenty is better known as a restaurant than a bar, but take it from us, on a midweek evening the small cocktail lounge overlooking Bleecker Street is a perfect place for relaxation. Its leather chairs, intimate lighting, and white walls covered in rich tapestries provide a perfect setting for quiet conversation. Also, during the summer, you can sit and drink in the spacious courtyard dining area ($4 minimum). However be warned: If you've got anything of an appetite you're going to find it hard to resist some of the fine dishes served here in the evening, particularly the soul food specialties—pork chitlins, smoked ham hocks, smothered chickens, and stuffed pork chops, all with homemade cornbread.

Horn of Plenty is the brainchild of David Williams, a young antique dealer who, with his partner David Black, first opened the place a few yards away across the street in 1970.

Due to various landlord problems and a plague of Village roaches (David even had to leave notes on the tables inviting guests to participate in nightly roach hunts) they moved to the present location in 1973. It's really a fine place. Service is admirable, table settings are superb, and as we noted, the cocktail lounge is a true delight so long as you don't visit on a hectic weekend evening.

JACQUE'S AT THE VILLAGE CORNER

ADDRESS: 142 Bleecker St. (at La Guardia Pl.); 473–9762
BAR HOURS: 11:30 A.M.–4 A.M.
FOOD: Hamburgers, etc. (inexpensive)
CREDIT CARDS: None
DRESS: Casual
SPECIAL FEATURES: Piano bar and darts
LIVELIEST TIMES: 9 P.M.–3 A.M. Thurs.–Sat.

To avoid confusion over the name of this pub we should point out that Jacque's, once located in the Greenwich Hotel, is now re-established at the Village Corner—dart boards, piano bar, and all. Owner Jim Smith points out that Jacque's may indeed return to its original location down the street when renovations at the hotel are complete. But meanwhile, darts fans and piano buffs must congregate at the Corner. And it's an odd but pleasant combination. Lance Hayward, a fine solo jazz pianist, plays each evening, except Wednesday, from 9:30 P.M.–3 A.M. while, in the front bar and back room, steady-armed dartists aim at "double-tops" and curse respectfully when their feathered missiles go astray.

The uninitiated customers gather around the bar itself, and gaze across the cigarette burns at Paris Webb, little realizing that this demure female is currently the New York women's darts champion and also a contender for the U.S. Darts Association Championship. Jim Smith claims this is the best bar in town for developing female darts players, regardless of the cryptic little note on the back-bar mirror that reads "Feminine or neuter pronouns shall be mentally substituted for those of a masculine gender"—it's a kind of last-ditch chauvinism. Paris Webb is a sign of things to come.

The crowd at the Corner is a typical Village-cosmopolitan mix, particularly at lunchtime when Jim's inflation-fighting combo of hamburger, French fries, and a drink (anything you wish) for under $2 is a good-enough bargain to attract the poorest student or the thriftiest Wall Streeter.

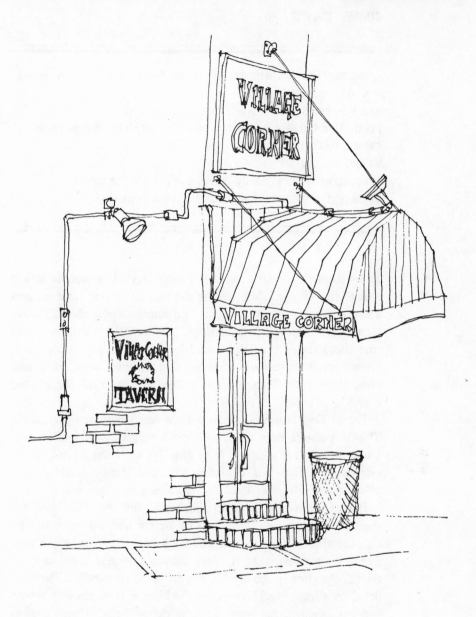

A final note: If you want to see some real darts playing, visit the Village Corner on Monday or Wednesday evenings when the local pub tournaments usually take place. And if you really want a bit of ego-puncture, challenge Paris Webb to a quick game of 301. Best of luck!

JIMMY DAY'S

ADDRESS: 192 W. 4th St. (between Sixth and Seventh aves.);
675–9793
BAR HOURS: 8 A.M.–4 A.M.; Sun. noon–4 A.M.
FOOD: Hamburgers, omelettes, etc., and specials (inexpensive)
CREDIT CARDS: None
DRESS: Casual
SPECIAL FEATURES: Daily brunch; cable TV for sports
LIVELIEST TIMES: Mid and late evenings Wed.–Sat.

In its short three-year existence, Jimmy Day's has become almost part of the Village fabric. In the summer its outdoor café attracts a continuous throng of residents and tourists doing the "Bleecker scene." During the winter months, however, the bar takes on its true character as a neighborhood locale and is particularly well known for its huge daily brunches that include bacon, ham, sausage, three eggs, French toast, coffee, and cocktail for a little over $3.

Jimmy Day himself, who is a little less world-weary than the Thakar portrait near the door would suggest, was once a bartender at WILLIE'S and is fully familiar with the legend of the elephant. In fact Willie Morrison helped Jimmy establish this place in the Village in 1972 and remains a loyal partner.

It's an unusually large establishment for the area, and the simple decor, entirely the work of Jimmy and his brother who also constructed the oval bar and back bar, is particularly attractive in the evening when the dark brown walls and green checked tablecloths glow in the light of a score of white candles. The food listed on a huge blackboard over the kitchen is generously served and inexpensive, the most popular dishes being Jimmy's omelette (containing an array of sliced cold cuts), chicken-in-a-basket, and the daily specials.

This was one of the first places in the Village to install cable TV for major sporting events. So, if you're looking for a quiet niche to spend an evening, avoid those sports nights and the weekends, which can get pretty hectic. However don't miss Jimmy's brunch.

JULIUS

ADDRESS: 159 W. 10th St. (at Waverly Pl.); 929–9672
BAR HOURS: 9 A.M.–4 A.M.; Sun. noon–4 A.M.
FOOD: Hamburgers, etc. (inexpensive)
CREDIT CARDS: None
DRESS: Very casual
LIVELIEST TIMES: Late evenings and weekends

This is one of the oldest remaining bars in the Village—the cobwebs and the local residents can both attest to that. If the owner hadn't put in a fireproof ceiling eight years ago, and in the process knocked down most of the webs, the place could have been dated like a tree—except instead of counting rings, you would have counted layers of dust.

Julius' history goes so far back no one can remember when it wasn't a hangout for local jazz musicians, sports stars, and even politicians. Today, you might still see your favorite quarterback gobbling a famous Julius hamburger while reading inscriptions on dozens of aging photographs of New York's past celebrities.

It's a friendly place and people all over the world have heard about it. Recently, some visiting French executives were so impressed with two of Julius' friendly bartenders that they treated them to two months touring France!

Julius is also known for its good, reliable drinks made with brand-name liquor. Its reputation in the area of drinks began even before prohibition, and like many places in the Village, continued despite the Volstead Act.

Some of the best stories about Julius come from people who have lived through a great part of its history. If you're lucky, maybe you'll run into Julius' new manager, Pat Fusci, a true Villager, or, possibly Leo Calarco, a local attorney, who can tell you about impromptu concerts by Fats Waller, where they hid the booze during the twenties, and visits by Truman Capote, Tennessee Williams, Rudolph Nureyev, and Bob Hope.

Always aware of the changing Village scene, the management of Julius is and was at the forefront in supporting the gay liberation movement. And now, in the afternoons and evenings, many

67

of the "liberated" patronize Julius. In fact, board meetings of *Dilettante,* a new nationwide magazine geared for the liberated audience, are held in Julius' chalk-scribbled back room.

But there is no reverse discrimination here and the gay scene is mild. If you just want to relax over a cool beer, sit in the back room away from the crowded bar and do your own thing. Everyone at Julius does just that and seems to enjoy it.

THE LION'S HEAD

ADDRESS: 59 Christopher St. (at 7th Ave.); 929–0670
BAR HOURS: Noon–4 A.M. daily
FOOD: American and specials (moderate)
CREDIT CARDS: None
DRESS: Casual
SPECIAL FEATURES: Sat. and Sun. brunch
LIVELIEST TIMES: 9 P.M.–1 A.M. most evenings

Al Koblin, who came to work at the Lion's Head as a bartender nine years ago and is now a partner, describes his clientele as "highly unlikely: Jewish drunks, Irish lovers, and Italian intellectuals." In the same breath, he also calls his patrons "middle class, middle age, and middle brow," and summarizes by saying they are actually middle class bohemians—making a living, but not leading a structured life. But he says all this with great affection, as he considers himself to be one of them, fitting into as many of his own categories as he can.

The two narrow rooms of the Lion's Head shelter separate crowds: the eaters and the drinkers. When you first walk down the stairs, after somehow managing to find this almost unmarked drinkers' haven, you're surprised that such a lively spot exists off this relatively quiet section of Christopher Street. But seated at the bar, you'll feel welcome, even as a stranger. There is a magnificent wooden lion's head over the center of the bar, which begins to look more and more ferocious after a few drinks. It is a replica of one in a banquet hall in England and comes from an insurance building in Newark that was torn down in 1908. While arguments often flurry over whether it is a male or female (we've heard some beauties!), it is certainly friendly, and has in its mouth a rubber lion cub, occasionally "squeaked" to signal closing time.

The Lion's Head has a reputation as a literary bar, but now the writers are mostly newspapermen. And Al says that while some claim it is a hangout for Norman Mailer and Jimmy Breslin, he's probably seen them a total of a dozen times during the past eight years.

The Lion's Head is really a neighborhood bar—the locals feel they can stay forever and then walk home. But the management doesn't play favorites. Al will hang up book jackets or posters that anyone brings in—as long as he agrees with their politics!

NO NAME BAR

ADDRESS: 621 Hudson St. (at Jane St.); 675–9640
BAR HOURS: Noon–4 A.M.
FOOD: Hamburgers and chili and impromptu specials (inexpensive)
CREDIT CARDS: Pending
DRESS: Casual
LIVELIEST TIMES: Late evenings and Sun. afternoons

Dan Lettieri, owner of No Name and one-time muscle man in Italian movies, looks for all the world like a true Sicilian godfather. In fact, on one of the walls of this tiny Village bar are photographs showing Dan in his auditioning outfit for that renowned film of Mafia machinations. Ironically, Dan's reputation stems more from his law-abiding qualities—he was awarded the Civilian Medal for protecting his customers from a particularly menacing gunman who once attempted to rob the bar.

It's a strange place, hard to categorize. Even on the brightest day, No Name is a dim enclave, its bar decor relieved only slightly by Peggy Lettieri's paintings on the wall opposite the bar. And yet it appears to attract a remarkably cosmopolitan crowd—actors (Jason Robards is a regular), local writers, members of the left-wing intelligentsia, and even a resident crank—who spends most evenings telling elaborate sea stories to five nonexistent companions.

Conversation here is often of a high caliber, even though Dan describes his bar top as "an altar of triviality." It's not everybody's choice of a place to spend an evening, but if you're feeling in the mood for a protracted discussion or wish to catch a glimpse of some theatrical celebrity in a natural setting, it's worth a visit.

1 IF BY LAND, 2 IF BY SEA

ADDRESS: 17 Barrow St. (between Seventh Ave. S. and W. 4th St.); 255–8649
BAR HOURS: 4 P.M.–4 A.M.
FOOD: American/European (expensive)
CREDIT CARDS: AE BA CB DC MC
DRESS: Mixed
SPECIAL FEATURES: Free hors d'oeuvres 4–8 P.M., entertainment by pianist
LIVELIEST TIMES: 9 P.M.–2 A.M. most evenings

Remember the address, for if you get lost in the Village and start asking directions to 1 If By Land, 2 If By Sea, even Villagers will look at you askance.

Once you find this delightful bar-restaurant, there will be no sign confirming your discovery. But press your nose to the window and you'll be amazed at what you see—it's almost like Alice dis-

covering Wonderland. And that's just what Armand Justin and Mario deMartini wanted: something a little different in the Village.

What they have created is a major artistic achievement. They have taken what was once a single-room Russian restaurant (originally Aaron Burr's Carriage House) knocked out its back wall, enclosed the courtyard that connected it to an abandoned two-story hayloft, rebuilt the hayloft, and decorated the entire structure inside with soft candlelight, tuxedoed waiters, original oil paintings by Mario, two fireplaces, rich carpeting, and a superb bar.

The changes were so monumental (and so subject to impromptu design modifications) that Armand and Mario had to do the job themselves over a period of two and a half years. They stripped the hayloft walls to the original brick and removed about four inches of tar and fifty coats of paint. They built a new floor in the hayloft and added wooden frames around the windows.

They removed false ceilings, six or seven walls, and excavated the whole basement. In doing so they found two tombstones and two vaults (according to rumor their ghostly occupants now haunt the place) and discovered what the local historical society claims was part of the "underground tunnel" that stretched all the way to the Hudson River and was used as part of a network for smuggling slaves out of the South and into the North during the Civil War era.

Almost without exception the bar is packed every evening, usually with an interesting cross section of gays and other Village residents. An elegant society matron, bejewelled and bedecked, may be sitting on a stool next to a young cavalier-haired artist in Levi's and, while the mood is generally subdued, the two may wind up together around the piano singing old favorites with the pianist who entertains every evening.

But 1 If By Land is not just a bar. It's a fine (and popular) restaurant featuring such dishes as individual beef Wellington, lime-broiled breast of capon, a huge portion of calves liver with bacon, and cracked king crab legs. If you're looking for something out of the ordinary in the Village, this is the place.

THE OTHER END

ADDRESS: 149 Bleecker St. (at La Guardia Pl.); 673–7030
BAR HOURS: Noon–4 A.M.
FOOD: Burgers, salads, omelettes, etc. (inexpensive)
CREDIT CARDS: None
DRESS: Casual
SPECIAL FEATURES: Folk music, $2.50 min. on Fri. and Sat. nights
LIVELIEST TIMES: After 9 P.M. on Tue. and weekends

Although the diminutive Paul Colby, part-owner of the Other End, is nearing retirement age, you wouldn't guess it. He never stops. The first time we met he was cramming a broiled cheese

73

sandwich into his walrus-moustached mouth, discussing the evening's schedule of live folk music with his ordained priest partner, Dale Lind, plugging an L.P. he recently produced ("The Bitter End Years") to two friends, and instructing a confused electrician on some new idea for stage lighting. It was not an easy interview.

Paul Colby and folk music are almost synonymous terms in the Village. He counts among his personal friends some of the most popular artists in the business and claims he was one of the first to recognize the potential of such superstars as James Taylor; Peter, Paul and Mary; Carly Simon—even Bill Cosby and Dick Cavett. That was in the old days when he was manager of the Bitter End until a disagreement with owner Fred Weintraub (producer of *Rage* and *Enter the Dragon*) convinced Paul to establish his own place, right next door. Ironically the Bitter End closed soon after and the Village lost not only a fine night spot, but a whole repertoire of those vast ice-cream concoctions for which the place was so renowned.

But all's well, etc. Paul has reopened the establishment and the big names in folk are back again—even the old brick wall at the rear of the stage, featured on countless albums covers, has been retained. Meanwhile he's kept the Other End as a popular showcase for lesser-known artists, who perform nightly from 10 P.M. to a young and enthusiastic audience. It's a warm, intimate place, complete with sawdust, red-check tablecloths, and walls plastered with old Bitter End posters for concerts by the Everly Brothers, Joni Mitchell, Tom Paxton, the Irish Rovers, Gordon Lightfoot, and Rick Nelson. There's even a large poster of Bill Haley for the true sentimentalists.

Weekends tend to be crowded, and Tuesday "talent" nights can be hectic. So, for a slower pace, come midweek and don't leave without trying the Boston clam chowder or spinach salad, two of the Other End's most popular snacks.

By the way, just down the street is another pleasant "showcase" kind of place, The Back Fence. It features lesser-known folk singers most evenings and has a lively following.

THE SAZERAC HOUSE

ADDRESS: 533 Hudson St. (at Charles St.); 989–0313
BAR HOURS: Noon–4 A.M.
FOOD: American and New Orleans (moderate)
CREDIT CARDS: AE BA DC MC
DRESS: Casual
SPECIAL FEATURES: New Orleans cuisine, chess
LIVELIEST TIMES: 8 P.M.–1 A.M. Wed.–Fri.

The West Village contains a few of the finest neighborhood pubs in the city, and the Sazerac House is certainly one of them. Pass by almost any afternoon and you'll see groups of bearded or bespectacled patrons poring intensely over worn chess boards, and maybe one or two huddled in a corner with a book from the Sazerac library by the window. It's that kind of place—small, clubby, and full of good fellowship.

The building is a notable landmark structure erected in 1826 for a local carpenter, Henry Bayard, on land originally part of a late eighteenth-century farm. During the following century it was used by a succession of artisans, and at one point by an Amsterdam diamond merchant. Little has changed. The building, with its Flemish bond brickwork and panelled lintels, is still an authentic structure, although owner Barry Cullen is striving to gain the Landmark Commission's blessing for a covered porch café—his pet project.

Inside, it's like an old London coffee house complete with working fireplace, booths with old wooden tables, tiny windows, and original brick walls. There's even a secluded alcove in the back, near the kitchen, where one could imagine Dr. Johnson delivering his latest thoughts and opinions to a captivated—or captive—audience.

Barry, once a bartender at CHUMLEY'S and part-owner of the popular Paris Bistro on Barrow Street, is justly proud of the New Orleans cuisine served here nightly—jambalaya, shrimp creole, plantation chicken, Louisiana crab chop, and flounder Pontchartrain—all excellent dishes and relatively inexpensive.

However, he warns light drinkers to avoid the Sazerac cocktail—a flamboyant and flammable mixture of bourbon, peychaud bitters, and high-proof absinthe.

While some gays and singles find this an attractive spot, the majority of the regulars are loyal and local residents.

SWEET BASIL

ADDRESS: 88 Seventh Ave. S. (between Grove and Bleecker Sts.);
   242–1785
BAR HOURS: 11 A.M.–4 A.M.
FOOD: Seafood, salads, omelettes (inexpensive)
CREDIT CARDS: AE, MC
DRESS: Casual
SPECIAL FEATURES: Live jazz 9 P.M.–1 A.M. Wed. and Thurs.,
   10 P.M.–2 A.M. Fri. and Sat., 6 P.M.–10 P.M. Sun.
LIVELIEST TIMES: Music hours

Although this fresh, sunlight-filled tavern only recently emerged from what used to be a renowned landmark of the area, the Village Drug Store, it has rapidly attracted a devoted following. The place is thronged most evenings and particularly on weekends, and it's not hard to understand the reasons. First, the food is "very Village" featuring some excellent fish dishes (shrimp creole, sole almondine, bass in cider), an interesting range of salads and omelettes, and a selection of vegetarian dishes for dietary purists. Second, the decor is simple yet sophisticated— unstained wood walls, carefully selected artwork and photographs, all under an old ornate tin ceiling. Third, and perhaps most important, owners Sherif Esmat and Dwain Tedford provide the finest live jazz in the evenings (Wed.–Sun.) with no cover charge and no minimum (at least not yet). It's remarkable how they can do it, particularly when the musicians include such well-known personalities as Ray Bryant, Jack Wilkins, Joe Puma, Ron Carter, and "Toots" Theilman.

When the Village Drug Store died after thirty-five years as an unpretentious but respected art and literary cultural center, many wondered dismally what could possibly take its place. Fortunately in Sweet Basil the Village has gained a notable successor and much of the old spirit has been retained. The bar is built of marble from the old counter, and occasionally the bean and noodle soup, for which the old establishment was so famous, is offered as a special.

77

and for
your further enjoyment...

ADAM & EVE (previously, Hungry Charlie's)

Waverly Place (at Mercer St.); 533–8380

Here's the Village version of a student beer hall complete with high brick walls, thick wooden tables, a cafeteria-style food counter, brimming pitchers of beer, and an always-lively crowd of young patrons from nearby N.Y.U. With the exception of a few huge blowups of old etchings, a large notice board full of posters and sale signs, and painted cast-iron pillars, the place has no notable decor. However, its friendly, club-like atmosphere makes it one of the most delightful watering holes in the area if you don't mind the absence of hard liquor.

ARTHUR'S TAVERN

57 Grove St. (at Seventh Ave. S.); CH 2–9468

Good old Arthur's Tavern—it'll never change. Most evenings Mabel Godwin is at the piano and blasts away with her powerful renditions of the "oldies but goodies" in this tiny, slightly faded little cocktail lounge. Monday evenings bring a change in mood and tempo when the Grove Street Stompers present a few exuberant hours of dixieland. The clientele tends to be a little older than usually found in Village taverns, but the atmosphere is friendly and connoisseurs of the Manhattan bar scene should not overlook this mini-landmark.

BROADWAY CHARLY'S

813 Broadway (at 11th St.); 477–9754

At first glance you'd probably dismiss Broadway Charly's as just another one of those interminable beer n' shot places. It has all the appropriate characteristics—flickering neon sign outside, pool table and yellow fluorescent lighting inside, tables covered with beer mugs, and a floor full of cigarette butts.

In actuality it's a lively neighborhood tavern catering to a cosmopolitan mix of truckers, students, artists, models, and writers. On a typical afternoon there'll be a huddle of students in the back room involved in ferocious debate, a bearded poet by the window scribbling on a pad, a group of warehousemen by the bar, and maybe a couple of well-dressed ladies at a table regarding the whole scene with ill-disguised amusement. Best times are music nights (Wed.–Sun. from around 9:30 P.M.) which feature live jazz or country and western music. Alternatively, come between 5 P.M. and 7 P.M. and enjoy a New York rarity— a 30¢ stein of beer.

BUFFALO ROADHOUSE

87 Seventh Ave. S. (at Barrow St.); 675–9875

What kind of name is that for a bar-restaurant? Apparently it's no kind of name. It's pure nonsense, according to Chris Powers and Gary Anderson, the two owners who five years ago transformed this ex-gas station into one of the most popular places in the mid-Village. During the summer (May–October) the outdoor patio is always crowded—tables brimming with beer mugs, great bowls of steamed clams, fat slices of quiche Lorraine, and omelettes. The kitchen stays open until 3 A.M. and the late-night drinking crowd includes an interesting selection of local writers and artists.

When the Village makes it back, it will be due in part to the imagination of people like Chris and Gary. They've created a truly pleasant, but unaffected place to while away a few hours in a part of the Village not previously noted for such attractions.

CASEY'S

142 W. 10th St. (off Greenwich Ave.); 255–5382

Casey's may sound like an Irish pub, but the resemblance ends there. For Casey is actually Kuo Ching Li (KC for short) and his bar-restaurant has become exactly what he intended: a fairly expensive, elegant place for "bohemians who don't want to get

dressed up." Notice the brick walls and archways of the former coach house (a series of superb ceramic masks by Jordan Stehel is currently on display), the fresh flowers, candles, and bright tablecloths on each immaculately laid table.

Not that Casey's elegance always inspires a quiet relaxed atmosphere. On the weekends particularly, the place attracts a large out-of-town clientele and the bar can get pretty boisterous. But the regulars feel at home here. Personal attention to detail by manager Keith Moorhead is certainly one of the reasons, and the French cuisine is excellent, featuring such dishes as striped bass in cream sauce with mushrooms, poulet Normandie au calvados, and roast duck with figs and wild rice.

THE DUGOUT TAVERN

145 Bleecker St. (at La Guardia Pl.); OR–4–5060

When the Village was at its height during the sixties young regulars came to the Dugout from as far afield as New Jersey and even Philadelphia, particularly when big names in folk singing were appearing at the adjacent Bitter End and other Bleecker Street clubs. There's still a young college crowd at the Dugout, many from neighboring N.Y.U.; but out-of-town trade dwindled along with the spirit of that lively era. Still, Friday and Saturday nights are often wild occasions here in this traditionally decorated pub—the sawdust flies and peanut shells lie inches thick in the early hours of the morning. There's plenty of life in the old place yet—and we mean old. The Dugout recently celebrated its twenty-five years of existence with a mammoth buffet for all its loyal patrons. Unfortunately, we missed it but promised to return for the fiftieth.

'55'

---

55 Christopher St. (at Seventh Ave.); 243-9332

If you really want a taste of raunchy Village drinking, pop into '55'—just up the street from the LION'S HEAD. No sign. No decor. Virtually no lighting. But this Bradley Cunningham place (BRADLEY'S) has what many Manhattan pubs have lost—true character, without the trimmings.

THE LOCALE

---

11 Waverly Pl. (at Mercer St.); 674-0860

Just across from ADAM & EVE is another delightful establishment catering mainly to many a Village crowd of actors, writers, and artists. Situated deep in the basement, it has an intimate club-like appeal. During winter months the roaring fire offers welcome respite from the cold winds across Washington Square.

A small but interesting selection of French and American dishes is offered in the carpeted dining room (hidden around the corner from the bar), but most of the action takes place in the area near the fireplace. Like many of the newer Village places, the Locale combines the spirit of a coffeehouse with the character of a true neighborhood pub.

MINETTA TAVERN

---

113 MacDougal Street (at Minetta Lane); 575–0845

The restaurant, well-known in the neighborhood for its Italian-European cuisine, is the main attraction here. It used to be headquarters for Joe Gould, one-time exponent of old-time bohemia in the Village, but today caters to a more urbane clientele.

The bar is a small (don't come with a crowd) but delightful niche. Its walls are decorated with caricature portraits by such cartoonists as Bernstein and Spencer, many of them browned with age. Above the bar and around the stained-glass liquor cabinets (a common feature in older New York bars) is a silhouetted frieze depicting Village life and boxing scenes, a favorite sport of Eddie Sieveri, past owner of the Tavern and once a fight referee himself.

PETER'S BACKYARD

---

64 W. 10th St. (at Sixth Ave.); 473–2400

Mario, the Backyard's bartender for almost twenty years, smiles as only an Italian can smile but keeps the stories of Peter's to himself. And this place, a Village "in" spot for over a decade, has many stories. Over in the corner, just past the piano, was Boris Karloff's favorite table. Humphrey Bogart used to frequent Peter's long before today's notables—Eugene McCarthy, Hugh Carey, Bette Midler, and Rex Reed—discovered the delightful dining rooms in the roofed-over "backyard."

The bar, once renowned as a singles spot, now caters to a slightly more heterogeneous crowd of Villagers. The Happy Hour, from 4:30 P.M. to 7 P.M. is a particularly popular time. After that, it tends to be taken over by anxious diners waiting for tables close to the barbecue pit which, according to maitre d' Sandy, was one of the first in New York.

It is a friendly, if slightly formal, place, and there's still enough action in the bar area to make it worth a visit.

ST. JAMES' INFIRMARY

22 Seventh Ave. (at Leroy St.); 675–1343

In its first few months of existence, this cramped basement establishment located in a nondescript part of the southern Village,

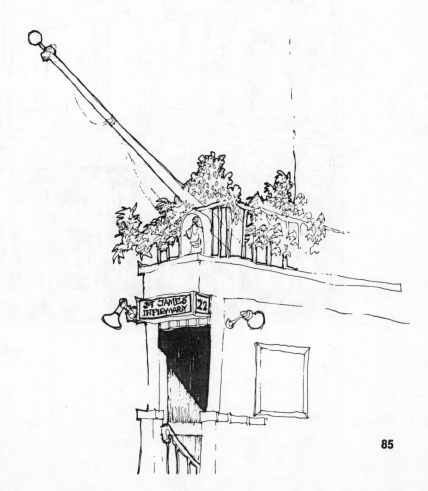

WHITE HORSE TAVERN

has attracted a remarkably loyal following by offering an excellent range of live jazz. Owner Hod O'Brien is a jazz pianist himself and accompanies many of the big names who appear regularly on the tiny stage—Chet Baker, Art Blakeley, Jimmy Giuffre, Roswell Rudd, and the versatile Dave Amram.

There's no cover and the $4 minimum is a modest price to pay for the music. But note: Weekends are often frantic here and it can get a little claustrophobic in the narrow, dark confines away from the bar. However, compared to many of the other, better-known jazz clubs in the Village, St. James' Infirmary offers outstanding value for the money. We hope it survives.

WHITE HORSE TAVERN

567 Hudson St. (at 11th St.); 243–9260

On a quiet day, a strong glass of Spaten München Beer and the slow swing of the grandfather clock's pendulum seems to send customers to sleep in this browned little tavern on the western fringe of the Village. But go in the early evening and you'll find it hard to get a seat in what used to be Dylan Thomas' favorite watering hole. The bar is out of a Western movie—huge fly-specked mirrors, yellowed with the cigarette smoke of decades and topped with the chipped plaster heads of white horses (the ones in the window are even more battered). But it's an interesting place full of quiet nostalgia—a truly authentic New York tavern.

THE WILLIAM SHAKESPEARE

176 MacDougal St. (at 8th St.); SP 7–2540

There are discoveries to be made at Shakespeare's: an interesting selection of people, Whitbread English beer, and nightly entertainment that can be outstanding (supported by passing the cup). Decorated à la English pub, the two rooms in Shakespeare's provide dining in the back and drinking and dining in the front. Here you can sip your beer and watch the Village street scene or admire the many posters featuring Shakespearean actors in various guises. There's usually a young, casual crowd, mostly from the Village, and late at night or on weekends the place is packed. At the bar, you can get 16-ounce mugs of beer for 80¢ each—a good buy. But if you want to sit at a table to sip, the price climbs to $1—still a good buy for a front-row seat at a show even Shakespeare himself would have appreciated.

GRAMERCY & VICINITY

In 1831 a farsighted real estate developer named Samuel Ruggles laid out Gramercy Park with all the residences facing inwards to a central park. His venture caused considerable amusement and skepticism among local residents. The wealthy mansion owners of Fifth Avenue whose carriage houses lined the small side streets as far east as Park Avenue, considered "the swamp" area, as it was then known, as even unfit for their horses. Residents of the stinking slums east of Third Avenue in the notorious "gas-house" district, were equally curious about the well-to-do tenants who used little gold keys to gain access to their private park, which they opened once a year to the public for carol singing. The whole development seemed a rather strange anomaly, but Mr. Ruggles' gamble paid off. Within a very short time, Gramercy Park became one of the most fashionable addresses in town. Edwin Booth's house and the Player's Club were located here and Samuel J. Tilden lived in what is now the National Arts Club after his unsuccessful bid for the Presidency in 1876.

Today Gramercy Park still remains as a fine and fashionable example of urban design, whereas most of the adjoining neighborhoods have undergone dramatic change. Fifth and Park avenues have long since lost their residences as commercial development moved steadily uptown. Many residents now live in the renovated carriage houses and side street brownstones. The 14th Street cultural scene with its Steinway Hall and Academy of Music has long since gone. The old Tammany Hall has been replaced by the Con Edison "Tower of Power" although Pete's Tavern, a favorite watering hole of the Tammany bosses, still remains, having flourished undisturbed through the prohibition era.

Perhaps the greatest change has taken place along the waterfront. The "gas-house" district, populated largely by Germans, Irish, and Ukrainians, had many of the characteristics of the ghetto areas surrounding the Bowery during its heyday as a gin mill and beer hall strip. Today all that remains are the Public Baths at 23rd Street and Asser Levy Place. Peter Cooper Village and Stuyvesant Town have obliterated every trace of that turbulent area. The local taverns—Guy Fawkes', Tuesday's, and Greensleeves reflect a younger, more prosperous clientele.

The same applies to the Kips Bay area, once a strong Irish enclave centered around the East River boat yards and today largely occupied by the Bellevue and Veterans' hospitals and E. M. Pei's Kips Bay Plaza apartments. Fortunately, there's still plenty of life left in the area centered around such establishments as Limerick's on Second Avenue, the Third Avenue taverns, and Timothy's Winery, surrounded by Indian food stores on Lexington Avenue.

Perhaps saddest of all the changes in the Gramercy district is the decline to anonymity of Madison Square. Not only are there no worthwhile pubs remaining in the area, but all life seems to have been drained from this once tingling district. The site of the great Madison Square Garden structure is now occupied by the New York Life building. The amazing Franconi's Hippodrome (1853), which seated over 10,000 spectators and featured Roman-styled pageants complete with gladiatorial contests and chariot races, has long since disappeared. Even the Square itself is a sad remnant of the original proposal for "The Parade," a vast park stretching between 23rd and 34th streets from Third to Seventh avenues.

However, there's one area that still lives up to all expectations and has for more than one hundred years boasted the densest concentration of Irish taverns outside Dublin. Third Avenue has long been a haven for serious drinkers. It's the area to avoid on St. Patrick's Day and to frequent when the rest of the city has retired for the night. In the days when the old Third Avenue "El" rumbled along the overhead tracks there were over 110 Irish taverns between 20th Street and 90th Street, and regular contests, official and unofficial, were held to see which stalwart character could drink his way furthest up the strip.

Although the avenue is somewhat smarter than in the old "El" days when adjoining neighborhoods were little better than ghettos for Irish and East European residents, the taverns still have that unmistakable brogue flavor. Most notable (as far north as 34th Street) are the Abbey Tavern, Connelly's, Glocca Morra, and

Molly Malone's. Connelly's in particular, is a charming, old-fashioned place that for a brief period was the local saloon for Butch Cassidy and the Sundance Kid before they embarked upon their South American adventures. Other places of interest in the same area include Caliban (with a special exit on the once notorious Broadway Alley), Company (a slightly gay-flavored bar-restaurant), the Good Times, and Once Upon a Stove. Finally, for a bar with a truly traditional Gramercy flavor there's Old Town tucked away up 18th Street off Park Avenue. It lacks the life of many of the better-known places but has a totally unspoiled charm, hard to find in Manhattan today.

THE ABBEY TAVERN

ADDRESS: 354 Third Ave. (at 26th St.); 532–1978
BAR HOURS: 11:30 A.M.–4 P.M.
FOOD: Irish/American (moderate)
CREDIT CARDS: AE DC
DRESS: Casual
SPECIAL FEATURES: Brunch after midnight daily and noon–5 P.M.
   Sat. and Sun.
LIVELIEST TIMES: 8P.M.–10 P.M. Wed.–Fri.

The Abbey is part of the JOHN BARLEYCORN/GREEN DERBY/FLANAGAN'S/BARRYMORE'S group and in common with the others has an intense Irish flavor. Manager Frank Burns is a former-steward from the *Queen Mary* (as are the owners of this group and many of their employees) and when we talked his eyes kept glancing over at the large painting of that magnificent liner hanging on the wall between the U.S. and Irish Republic flags.

The crowd here varies considerably. At lunchtime it's mainly professionals from nearby offices, but in the evening there's a sizeable singles contingent mixed with the older regulars. The day barman, Mike O'Connor (previously with DOWNEY'S for fifteen years), has a smile and a wink for everyone—and a repertoire of bar tales and stories matched only by the true greats in the business including Frank Conefrey (P. J. CLARKE'S) and John Gallagher (COSTELLO'S). Austin White, the evening barman, is an equally outstanding individual with a prodigious memory for faces, names, and the drinks that go with them. Characters such as these are rare in New York today and give the Abbey a particularly unique flavor.

Of course there's serious drinking here too under the Tiffany lamps, old Irish whiskey jugs, and pewter pots that hang from the ceiling beams. For beer lovers there's draft Guinness, Harp, and Bass. If you prefer something a little stronger, try the Irish martini made from Cork dry gin or the nonblended Glenfiddick Scotch.

CALIBAN

ADDRESS: 360 Third Ave. (between 26th and 27th sts.); MU 9–
5155
BAR HOURS: Noon–3 A.M.
FOOD: Mainly American (expensive)
CREDIT CARDS: AE BA CB DC MC
DRESS: Casual
SPECIAL FEATURES: Brand name "pouring" drinks, splendid wine
list
LIVELIEST TIMES: 10 P.M.–2 A.M. weekends

"We somehow never got around to it" was owner Harry Marten's nebulous response to our curiosity about the lack of any exterior sign for Caliban. "However, we did put a plaque on the door a couple of years ago." We checked. He's right—but its 12 square inches must make it the smallest bar sign in the city, excluding such notoriously elusive places as CHUMLEY'S and 1 IF BY LAND in the Village, which have no signs at all.

Caliban's somewhat insular atmosphere is even further emphasized during the day when the partial-mirror windows facing the street block any view of the pubs interior. It's such a pleasant change to find a place that doesn't flaunt itself.

This same spirit of sophisticated restraint is echoed inside the large high ceilinged space with bare brick walls, old wooden floorboards, worn tables (ideal for the afternoon chess-and-chat crowd), and a superb bar originally made for the Knickerbocker Brewing Company. Harry and friends moved it here piece by piece from an old Duane Street saloon.

At the time of our visits Harry was finalizing plans to convert the rear patio into an extension of the dining area with a special entrance off the rear alley. And thereby hangs a tale. This narrow, unimposing little street was once the notorious "Broadway Alley" —a kind of mini-Tenderloin complete with bordellos, girly shows, bars of dubious reputation, and a remarkably high murder rate Harry even wonders about trying to re-create the alley scene— with modifications of course. But so far local interest is not particularly pronounced.

93

Without doubt, Caliban is an establishment of good taste. Take a look at the wine list. In addition to an excellent selection of French vintages, Harry is a connoisseur of California wines, and many of that state's small, top-flight wineries, unfamiliar to most East Coast residents, are given well-deserved prominence. If the place isn't too hectic, ask to see the temperature-controlled wine cellars located in the vaults of what used to be a basement pawn shop.

The cuisine is also outstanding, particularly the appetizers of freshly made quiche, crêpes Alexandre, and mussels in white wine; entrées such as shrimp provençale, trout almondine, veal crown bual, and chicken cordon bleu; and a selection of desserts including baked Alaska (for four).

It's often the little things—the care for details—that make a good bar or restaurant. At Caliban, wine is served at just the right temperature, the house Burgundy is Heitz, real roquefort is used in the salad dressing, and all "pouring" drinks are top-flight brand names. This place has true class.

COMPANY

ADDRESS: 365 Third Ave. (at 27 St.); MU 3–9033
BAR HOURS: Noon–4 A.M.
FOOD: Varied (expensive)
CREDIT CARDS: AE BA CB DC MC
DRESS: Casual
SPECIAL FEATURES: Cocktail hour with free buffet and 2-for-1
    drinks, midnight brunch 12:30 A.M.–3 A.M. Fri. and Sat.
LIVELIEST TIMES: Buffet time and late evenings Wed.–Sat.

You may remember Company as the place that gave away free T-shirts on the night of its first anniversary and attracted such a crowd that police had to set up special barricades to keep traffic moving on Third Avenue. It also gained a somewhat dubious reputation for holding Manhattan's first (and probably last) "porno-party" which introduced streaking to the city.

Regardless of such past events, it's a delightful place, well loved by Manhattan's gay community, but gentle enough to attract a more diversified clientele, including a strong theatrical following. Decor is simple but tasteful—white plaster walls dotted with framed theatre posters, small tables lit by red, amber, and blue spotlights. The Rear End room, located as one might expect at the back of the restaurant, boasts a fine collection of posterior paintings and lithographs; it could be crass but it's not.

At the time of our visits, Jeff Croland (one-time salad man, D.J., and broadcast-time salesman) and his partner, Chuck Cardillo, were in the process of transforming the rear patio into a dining/cabaret spot and supper club. We only hope that this expansion does not affect the quality of Company's cuisine, which includes a varied selection of dishes all cooked to order—chicken suprême (once featured on ABC's "Eyewitness News"), stuffed pork chop, chicken Kiev, shrimp New Orleans, curries, etc.

Just a word of warning. The bar section is rather small and on the busy evenings (Wed.–Sat.) it's usually taken up by groups waiting for tables. So if you're looking for a quieter scene, come early in the week.

CONNELLY'S

ADDRESS: 299 Third Ave. (at 23rd St.); 686–9643
BAR HOURS: 8 A.M.–11 P.M.
FOOD: American/Irish (moderate)
CREDIT CARDS: AE BA CB DC MC
DRESS: Informal
SPECIAL FEATURES: "Leprechaun" after-dinner drink, inexpensive
    counter lunch
LIVELIEST TIMES: Varies but usually mid-evenings late in the
    week

When the trains rumbled and squeaked along the elevated tracks above Third Avenue and filtering shafts of sunlight pierced the dim gloom of a hundred Irish bars between 20th and 90th streets, Connelly's was one of the most popular establishments in

95

the area. It was particularly renowned for its fine lunch counter and American/Irish dishes of lamb stew, pot roast and red cabbage, spare ribs, and Dublin bay prawns.

Since then the El has gone, many of the old taverns—Lennon's, Sullivan's, Dunleavy's, Murphy's—are merely names in the memories of the older residents, and the street scene with its occasional high rise apartments, reflects a rapidly changing neighborhood. But Connelly's remains. The lunch counter, dark wood panelling, brass trimmings, the hunting mural above the bar— even the menu (including those exquisite Dublin bay prawns)— have all been carefully preserved by Gene Connelly, son of Tom Connelly from Sligo, Ireland (who owned the bar from 1914, with a slight interruption during prohibition). Here's one older place for a change that doesn't possess a speakeasy history—score one for Carry Nation.

Of course a few things have changed. Connelly's is no longer an all male bar and a haven for the political-club crowd. Evenings, particularly Thursdays and Fridays, attract an interesting mix of young locals, businessmen, and occasional theatrical celebrities. Bill Riley, former Irish football star and ex-director of elections for De Valera claims it's the best place for quiet socializing on this stretch of Third Avenue. Allowing for his bias, we agree that Connelly's has an old-fashioned, noncommercialized charm and fine restaurant that offers respite from the "bouncing track" bars further uptown. And it's full of history (note the old El waiting room stove just by the door). In fact, recent research has uncovered the fact that Connelly's was a bar popular with the Butch Cassidy and Sundance Kid team who lived briefly in the area before leaving for their robbery-romp through South America.

GLOCCA MORRA

ADDRESS: 304 Third Ave. (at 23rd St.); 473–9638
BAR HOURS: 11:30 A.M.–4 A.M.
FOOD: Irish/American (inexpensive)
CREDIT CARDS: None
DRESS: Casual
SPECIAL FEATURES: Darts tournaments on Tues.; live music, 10
    A.M.–4 A.M. Wed.–Sun.
LIVELIEST TIMES: 9 P.M.–3 A.M. Tues.–Fri.

Here's another fine darts bar. It's been in existence for over four years and has all the brisk Irish flavor one expects in this part of town including a fine selection of imported draft ales— Bass, Guinness, Harp, and an interesting array of American and Irish dishes usually listed on the various blackboards around the place.

In common with other darts bars in the city, Tuesday nights bring the big league teams and their followers, huddling and milling around the two boards placed at opposite ends of the bar. But Glocca Morra has another attraction—live Irish and country music, Wednesday through Sunday 10 P.M. to closing time. **97**

It's a leisurely, easy kind of place, popular both with singles and professional elbow-benders. The decor is pleasant—old flags, photographs of football teams long since disbanded, maps, dusty farm implements—but it's the people that make the place. Try and pop in when Jim Costello is tending bar (another member of that extensive family—see review of COSTELLO'S). He's got tales galore about the place and the neighborhood and even though he keeps talking about returning to his teaching profession at the John Jay College of Criminal Justice, he somehow looks like a permanent fixture.

One last note. If you've never seen good female darts throwers in action, give Jim a call and ask him when the Glocca Morra's "Darter's Lib" team is playing. It's one of the few all-female teams in Manhattan and well worth watching.

THE GOOD TIMES

ADDRESS: 449 Third Ave. (at 31st St.); 679–9077
BAR HOURS: 11 A.M.–4 A.M.
CREDIT CARDS: AE BA MC
FOOD: American (moderate)
DRESS: Informal
SPECIAL FEATURES: Piano bar, hot hors d'oeuvres 5 P.M.–7 P.M.
    Mon.–Fri.; brunch daily after midnight and Sun.
LIVELIEST TIMES: 9 P.M.–2 A.M. Thursday and Friday

It was the building itself that first caught our attention—a tall, thin structure standing alone, looking as if one hearty gust of wind down the avenue would send it sprawling into the adjoining parking lot. However, as manager Jim Colucci told us, the place has withstood a number of traumas, including a severe fire that gutted the previous bar, Clan 1890's, and led to the recent name and decor change. Singles will remember the old place well, famous for its free peanuts, Victorian decor, and regular performances of Ron Denner's "bar-theatre"—a miscellany of acts including singers, magicians, raconteurs, and musicians.

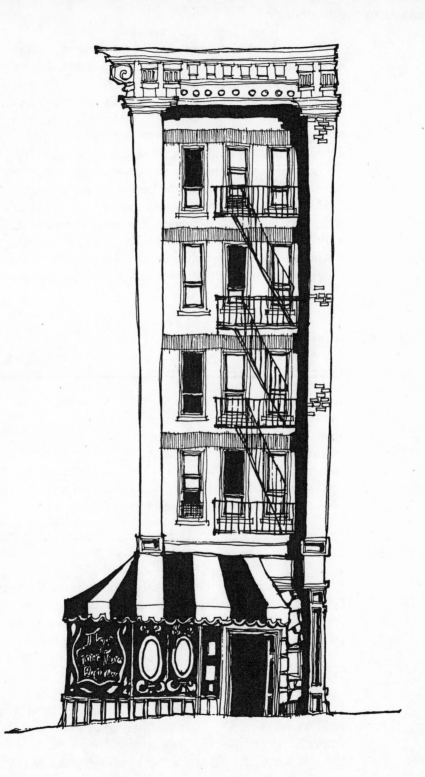

It all looks very different today—more like a Mediterranean café complete with white plaster walls and arches, delicate paintings, canvas restaurant chairs, and coy vistas of the streets and passing scene through oval windows. It's still popular with the singles, although new groups are appearing, including regular contingents of prominent athletes and their followers. Some nights, particularly Fridays, it's frankly too popular. We prefer the cocktail hour during the quieter weeknights when patrons munch on hot hors d'oeuvres and enjoy the piano bar.

Although there's a spacious area reserved for serious drinkers, and plenty of room for intimate, one-to-one conversation, Good Times has gained a sound reputation for its simple but hearty food (including a whopping half-pound hamburger with all the trimmings) and the brunch is served not only on Sunday but every evening starting around midnight.

GREENSLEEVES

ADDRESS: 543 Second Ave. (at 30th St.); 679–9556
BAR HOURS: 11:30 A.M.–3 A.M.
FOOD: American and European (moderate)
CREDIT CARDS: None
DRESS: Casual
SPECIAL FEATURES: Cable TV for sporting events
LIVELIEST TIMES: 9 P.M.–midnight Thurs.–Sat.

Note the sketches in this pub. Many of them are the work of Charles Spiess, who owns Greensleeves in addition to moonlighting as a professional architectural renderer. In its eight years of existence, the pub has become one of the most popular meeting places in the neighborhood, attracting a cross section of mostly young, local residents.

Charles, regarded by many of his customers as something of a Renaissance man, also designed the place and is one of its principal dinner chefs. The front oval bar with its fan-like ceiling is particularly attractive and well separated from the rear dining room, which is cleverly broken up by wrought iron and stained-

100

glass screens into small intimate niches. There's hardly one table where you wouldn't feel comfortable and secluded, and the "romantic-chintz" decor, complete with shuttered windows, shingle walls, and Tiffany-type lamps provides an admirable setting for the rich, continental cuisine served here. Particularly popular are the veal and chicken dishes, especially the excellent saltimbocca alla Romana (veal slices with prosciutto and Marsala sauce) and the chicken Mornay on broccoli.

The bar has a distinct scene of its own and the same young regulars gather here every night to create an atmosphere of warmth and conviviality.

GUY FAWKES

ADDRESS: 365 First Ave. (between 21st and 22nd Sts.); 475–9563

BAR HOURS: 11 A.M.–4 A.M.

FOOD: Hamburgers, etc. (inexpensive)

CREDIT CARDS: None

DRESS: Casual

SPECIAL FEATURES: Live Irish and country music (9 P.M.–4 A.M. Fri. and Sat.)

LIVELIEST TIMES: Wed.–Sat. 10 P.M.–4 A.M.

For those who remember their high school history, Guy Fawkes was the resolute fellow who unsuccessfully attempted to demolish England's Houses of Parliament with his gunpowder plot on November 5, 1605. Appropriately enough, this small but well-loved pub has its own wild Halloween-type celebration every November 5 (Guy Fawkes Day in England), and although we're not suggesting you put off your visit to that date, try not to miss the event.

Of course there are other attractions at this pleasant tavern, which looks more like a British pub than many British pubs. Every Wednesday is a true beer night when brimming steins cost a mere 25¢ apiece and seem to attract almost every student and nurse in the neighborhood. Alternatively, come on Tuesdays and watch the darts tournaments in process. On our last visit the Guy Fawkes team had just tied with Manhattan's true virtuosos—the SOHO DARTS BAR team and there was a celebration that night that will long be remembered by the participants (or at least those who survived). If neither Tuesday nor Wednesday are good drinking nights for you, pop in during the live Irish and country music sessions (9 P.M. to closing time Fri. and Sat.).

There always seems to be something going on down at Guy Fawkes. However those preferring a quieter evening should come on Mondays and sit in the back room with its old-fashioned raised booths—ideal for intimate conversation. Just make sure there's no major sporting event on though, otherwise the management may offer one of its "eat and drink all you can" orgies. At the last there were over 300 fans crammed around the cable TV set, and the beer consumed that evening was enough to drain a brewery.

LIMERICK'S

ADDRESS: 573 Second Ave. (at 31st St.); 683–4686
BAR HOURS: 11:30 A.M.–1 A.M.
FOOD: English/Irish and American (moderate)
CREDIT CARDS: AE BA CB DC MC
DRESS: Casual
SPECIAL FEATURES: Sun. brunch 11:30 A.M.–4 P.M.
LIVELIEST TIMES: Wed.–Fri. 6 P.M.–10 P.M.

Many of the bars in the Kip's Bay area reflect its once-predominantly Irish character, although recent redevelopment and an influx of young professionals has led to considerable change in the neighborhood.

Limerick's has been around for almost ten years. It began as a tiny one-room pub but subsequently expanded into a long bar-restaurant with a charming outdoor patio. Fortunately the Irish flavor was not lost in the process. John Garvey, the barman-raconteur, is proud of his selection of native draft beers—Harp, Guinness, and Bass Ale—and the menu reflects the best in English and Irish cuisine—steak and kidney pie, Irish stew, bangers 'n' mash, fish 'n' chips, and prawns in beer batter—all served with homemade soda bread.

The crowd consists mainly of regular local residents and the place is warm and friendly, especially when John Garvey is in top form with his jokes and anecdotes. The previous barman, Joe McSteifer, left a couple of years ago to open the Animal Gourmet—that strange establishment at 19 E. 65th Street where dewey-eyed matrons bring immaculately adorned poodles to feast on Cordon Bleu dishes (at Cordon Bleu prices). In his quieter moments behind the bar, John occasionally wonders if he's in the right job . . . .

MOLLY MALONE'S

ADDRESS: 287 Third Ave. (between 22nd and 23rd sts.);
    686–9550
BAR HOURS: 11:30 A.M.–4 A.M.
FOOD: American/Irish (moderate)
CREDIT CARDS: AE BA DC MC
DRESS: Casual
SPECIAL FEATURES: Sunday brunch (featuring Irish sausage and
    and bacon), cocktail hour with hot hors d'oeuvres
LIVELIEST TIMES: most evenings

From the tales of Brendan Behan's escapades in New York, it's amazing that the flamboyant Irish playwright ever had time or energy to put pen to paper. Hence it was interesting to meet Norman Purfield, owner of this fine Irish tavern, who gives a more rounded picture of the misunderstood man. Of course, if you're looking for the typical Behan story he'll provide it; but at the same time, he likes to remind his amused listeners that Brendan was a man of enormous sensitivity and intelligence and one of the most considerate Irish notables ever to make his mark in this city. According to Norman, who lived in Dublin on the adjoining street to the Behan family, Brendan was rarely without an encouraging word or generous buck for struggling writers, and his bouts with the bottle stemmed mainly from his somewhat turbulent childhood.

Molly Malone's has a most convivial atmosphere. The bar always seems busy in the early evening when free hors d'oeuvres are available and attract a wide variety of customers—from art students to newspaper journalists and theatricals. In the winter it's particularly cozy around the old fireplace (which Norman claims dates from the late 1600s when the building was a farmhouse). The orange glow lights up the ceiling beams and catches the framed lithographs and old maps that adorn the walls along with a collection of Irish whiskey jugs. In common with many of the pubs in the vicinity, Molly Malone's features a good selection of Irish and American dishes including pork chops with apple fritters, calves liver and bacon, shepherd's pie, and Irish lamb stew —all served with homemade soda bread.

ONCE UPON A STOVE

ADDRESS: 325 Third Ave. at 24th St.) ; 683–0044
BAR HOURS: 5 P.M.–midnight
FOOD: Varied (moderate)
CREDIT CARDS: AE BA CB DC MC
DRESS: Informal
SPECIAL FEATURES: Decor and atmosphere, cocktail hour
    5 P.M.–6:30 P.M.
LIVELIEST TIMES: Wed.–Sat. 6 P.M.–10 P.M.

Owner Hank Sgrosso has been collecting roomfuls of odds and ends and bric-a-brac for years and finally he's found a place to put them all. Once Upon a Stove is a delightful maze full of hidden rooms and corners, often crammed to the ceiling with antiques and all forms of assorted objects—chandeliers, musical instruments, battered paintings, ship's lamps, cartwheels, figureheads, bits and pieces of brass beds—there's no way to describe

105

the profusion of artifacts that abound here. You'll have to come and see for yourself.

If you do that, bear in mind that there are two entrances. The main Third Avenue door leads directly past the "antique shop" into the front dining room. If you keep on going, you'll eventually find the bar in what used to be an old church. In fact, if you look closely enough you'll see that the elaborate back bar was once a confessional—and in some respects, with some of the clients, it still is.

The second entrance, more convenient for the bar, is off 24th Street. Coming in this way you receive the full impact of the remodelled church. It's a beautifully rich space, complete with dining booths, galleries, and a staircase at the far end that leads up to an even more exotic dining room in a kind of French baroque-with-frills style. To add to its bizarre spirit, this upstairs room also features singing waitresses in continuous impromptu cabaret—a sort of midtown Asti's.

The bar attracts a mixed crowd—mainly young—and is particularly popular around the cocktail hour (5 P.M.–6:30 P.M., hot and cold hors d'oeuvres are available), and also during the later evening.

One last note. Almost everything displayed in this unusual establishment is for sale so, if you decide to dine here (and the food is generally good—particularly the appetizers), don't be surprised if Hank comes up and quietly asks if he may take your chair to complete a set.

PETE'S TAVERN

ADDRESS: 129 E. 18th St. (at Irving Pl.); GR 3–7676
BAR HOURS: 11:30 A.M.–midnight Sun.–Thurs., 11:30 A.M.–
    1 A.M. Fri. and Sat.
FOOD: Italian and American (moderate)
CREDIT CARDS: AE BA CB DS MC
DRESS: Casual
SPECIAL FEATURES: The O. Henry booth
LIVELIEST TIMES: 7 P.M.–10 P.M. Wed.–Sat.

It's a shame we didn't start this project a little earlier—before Joe Negri passed away. He was the bartender at Pete's Tavern for forty years (his uncle was the original Pete), and when he died, he not only took the recipe for "The Lost Blend" (a Pete's Tavern special drink), but he also took most of the great old stories of Pete's history with him. The present owner, Helen Frawley, claims she hardly knows the place at all—she's only been there a mere seventeen years!

The tavern opened in 1864 and claims to be the oldest continually operating establishment in the city. As with many of the other equally renowned landmark bars, it had its notorious speakeasy phase when patrons entered through the refrigerator in the flower store used to disguise the tavern's true purpose. Ironically, the store itself was a highly profitable venture, serving wealthy customers from the Gramercy Park area, and according to one of the locals there were quite a few problems in ousting the tenant after the repeal of prohibition.

Way back in its long history, Pete's was the local hangout for the Tammany Hall politicians and influence-peddlers. At that time, the Hall was located a little farther along Irving Place at 14th Street, and many of the shady deals concocted within its walls were consummated at the long rosewood bar (a replica of which can be found at Shepherd's at the Drake Hotel) or in the intimate booths that still line one side of the tavern area. By the way, note the first booth as you enter the main doorway. It was here that O. Henry wrote his "Gift of the Magi"—so at least Pete's has some respectable history.

Even though the tavern has retained much of its character, there have been many changes. The rear stables have been converted into an attractive restaurant that features an interesting selection of Italian and American dishes. It's packed, particularly at lunch times, and in the evenings the bar attracts a young crowd from the neighborhood and nearby hospitals. Fortunately this doesn't seem to keep the older regulars out—they still regard the bar as their exclusive territory during the day, and on Friday afternoon members of local union organizations often flood the place, bringing back memories of the old Tammany days to this fine Manhattan landmark.

TIMOTHY'S WINERY

ADDRESS: 127 Lexington Ave. (between 28th and 29th sts.); 532–7674
BAR HOURS: 11:30 A.M.–1 A.M.; closed Sun.
FOOD: Thai and American (moderate)
CREDIT CARDS: None
DRESS: Casual
SPECIAL FEATURES: Beer garden and clam bar (summers only)
LIVELIEST TIMES: 8 P.M.–11 P.M.

Timothy Remy and his wife, Roberta, have created a masterpiece in Timothy's Winery. The sketch (prepared by Roberta, whose artwork is also displayed on the walls of the upstairs dining room) reflects the intimate Mediterranean atmosphere of the cellar bar-restaurant. At the far end is the canopy-enclosed patio. In the summer months it's full of hanging plants bathed in shafts of sunlight, and patrons while away the warm evening hours over steins of cold Spaten München beer and fresh clams, served from the clam bar.

109

Upstairs is a delightful high-ceilinged dining room with a small raised area by the window—a favorite spot with the locals. Timothy preserved the old plaster-molded beams, used the walls to display paintings by his wife and other neighborhood artists, and, again, filled the room with a host of hanging plants. Behind the ornate cupboard at the rear of the room is the kitchen where Oriental chefs prepare the Winery's unusual dishes—chicken gai yang, hot Thai beef salade, chicken breasts shi pao li, calamari with red wine sauce, and grilled Thai shrimp. Those familiar with the neighborhood will remember when Timothy's was famous for its French food and wine cellar. However, as tastes (and affluence levels) changed and younger residents moved into the area. Timothy decided to switch to a shorter and simpler menu. It worked

110

wonders and the place rapidly gained a loyal, local following. Downstairs around the bar are photographs of some of the regulars, including "Mike the Greek"—one of the neighborhood's most notable characters.

Timothy's is full of little surprises. There's always a large basket of dark "Bistro Loaves" by the bar available to everyone. The ornate bar was found lying in a snow-covered field on Long Island. There's a chess table near the door (invariably occupied), surrounded by some most distracting photographs of satirically posed nude females. It's really a most unusual but enjoyable place.

TUESDAY'S

ADDRESS: 190 Third Ave. (at 17th St.); 533–7900
BAR HOURS: 11:30 A.M.–4 A.M.
FOOD: Hamburgers, steak, salads, etc. (inexpensive)
CREDIT CARDS: AE DC MC
DRESS: Informal
SPECIAL FEATURES: Decor and downstairs discotheque ($5 minimum), brunch noon–4:30 P.M. Sat. and Sun.
LIVELIEST TIMES: Wed.–Sat. 9 P.M.–midnight

Here's another Alan Stillman, Ben Benson, and Ernie Kalman creation—this one dripping with Victorian atmosphere and full of beautiful people. In terms of decor, nothing has been missed, from the old-fashioned glass windows facing onto the street to the palms, sepia photographs, Tiffany lamps, huge mirrors in great gilded frames, and a hundred other objets d'art of which Stillman and Benson seem to possess an infinite supply.

Tuesday's is a comparative newcomer to the scene (it arrived four years after FRIDAY'S) and is a little different from the other singles places farther uptown. It was originally Joe King's Rathskeller and photographs of that famous light heavyweight champion adorn many of the walls both in the main bar and down-

111

stairs in Tuesday's Bottom—primarily a discotheque and enclave for the singles. In contrast, the main bar-restaurant attracts a neighborhood crowd and the "meat rack" characteristics, a little overpowering uptown, are replaced by a mature ambiance and friendly atmosphere that comes with a regular clientele who know and like one another. The menu is similar to FRIDAY'S and the fish n' chips are outstanding.

**and for
your further enjoyment...**

DENO'S

157 E. 26th St. (at Third Ave.); 725–9386

Although Deno's is primarily a fascinating complex of restaurants, there's a small bar in the Victorian-styled corner dining room—just past the unusual "Penny Candy Store." It's hidden behind a glass and bead screen and is usually used by patrons waiting to eat. However, it's a rather unique place for a drink if you avoid the dinner crush.

KENWALL

129 Lexington Ave. (between 28th and 29th sts.); 684–8832

Next door to TIMOTHY'S WINERY is this small, old-fashioned tavern catering to an older neighborhood crowd. If you'd like to experience a little of the Lexington atmosphere as it used to be, this is a fine place to stop for a drink, particularly if "Mike the Greek" is around. He's one of those special neighborhood characters everyone seems to love.

MUNK'S PARK

379 Park Ave. S. (between 26th and 27th sts.); 679–3838

The old English/Irish decor is great—stags' heads, old gilded mirrors, tile floor, paintings and lithographs—in a large, high-ceiling room. Unfortunately Munk's Park, located in a somewhat dull part of Park Avenue, caters primarily to a lunchtime crowd, and evenings are occasionally quiet in the extreme. It's a shame. The place has character, and the neighborhood has few other pubs of this quality. However, Monday nights are usually the exception. The old Bells of Hell crowd from the Village has moved its weekly Irish "seisiun" up here, so if you're into folk songs, Irish music, poetry, fairy tales, or any of the other related characteristics of a good seisiun, this is your kind of place. Give it a try.

OLD TOWN

45 East 18th St. (between Park Ave. S. and Broadway); 477–9794

Here's a fine old-fashioned tavern complete with ornate tin ceiling, a magnificent back-bar (one of the largest in the city), intimate dark-wood booths lit by brass and glass lanterns, and a white tile floor, once a traditional feature of Manhattan's older taverns.

Old Town is kept in magnificent condition and were it located in a more residential sector of the island, would doubtless attract hordes of devoted patrons. As it is, the place is usually rather quiet and caters primarily to local businessmen and truckers. There are no gimmicks here, no pandering to "upbeat" styles and tastes. It's simply a perfect example of a late nineteenth-century tavern that's been owned by the same family for almost ninety years, and we hope it remains that way.

MIDTOWN WEST & CHELSEA

There is no better district to illustrate E. B. White's description of New York: "Each area is a city within a city within a city." Midtown west is without doubt the most diverse sector of Manhattan, combining on the one hand the quiet brownstone streets of Chelsea around the General Theological Seminary and on the other, the raucous, neon-lit, erotic "combat-zone" of Times Square and 42nd Street between Sixth and Eighth avenues. In between lie a host of mini-districts all with their own unique characteristics, customs, and traditions.

It all began rather quietly in 1750, when Captain Thomas Clarke purchased a pleasant estate along the Hudson River between 14th and 27th streets. In 1830, his grandson, Clement Clarke Moore (noted biblical scholar and author of the famous poem "The Night Before Christmas"), subdivided and sold most of the estate for an elegant town house development named after London's fashionable, residential district, Chelsea.

Typical of New York's historical growth pattern, the elegance was marred by the erection of slum tenements for mainly Irish inhabitants along the rapidly industrializing Hudson River, and the construction of the Ninth Avenue El in 1871. The eastern sector of Chelsea, however, which possessed one of the city's first cooperative apartment buildings (remodelled in 1905 as the Chelsea Hotel and famous for its literary tenants—O. Henry, Thomas Wolfe, Dylan Thomas, and Brendan Behan—maintained its elite character until the construction of the Sixth Avenue El. Then the emergence of the "Tenderloin District" around 1900—a Bowery-styled strip of bordellos, bars, and dance houses centered around Sixth Avenue north of 14th Street—brought about a decline from which the area has only recently recovered. Chelsea streets are being renovated and taverns such as West Boondock, the Angry Squire, and R. J. Scotty's are indicative of a promising renaissance.

The Clinton district to the north, once known as Hell's Kitchen the city's most notorious slum, is also on the upsurge. The most notable feature here is the fascinating Paddy's Market around Ninth Avenue and 40th Street with Giordano's restaurant and bar located in the heart of the hubbub. Also nearby is the recently opened Landmark Tavern—another indication of the neighborhood's revival.

But it's the vibrant mini-districts for which midtown is so renowned. Lower down on Sixth Avenue there's the flower market, centered around 28th Street—a marvelous place for an early morning stroll with its jungle-like sidewalks filled with blooms, bushes, and blossoms. Immediately adjoining is the fur district with its murky little storefront windows packed with skins of every texture and color. To the north, centered around Seventh Avenue and 38th Street, is the frenzied garment district. Originally the tailors and milliners were located in an equally compact area in the heart of downtown, before they moved en masse to their present location—a complex, self-contained rabbit warren of factories, wholesale outlets, snack bars, synagogues, and tiny stores. During the day activity in the narrow streets never ceases. Trucks, filled with bales of cloth, line the sidewalks; porters push long racks of half-finished garments from one cramped factory to another; the buzz and whirl of ten thousand sewing machines fill the streets.

The equally integrated jewelry district is situated around 47th Street between Fifth and Sixth avenues. Behind the glossy store front exteriors lies another maze of tiny rooms and passages where the real work of cutting, cleaning and setting is done. The pace never ceases. Yiddish-speaking salesmen and merchants throng the sidewalks arguing, cajoling, bargaining, and smiling those little secret smiles as they watch potential patrons ogle at the displays of diamonds, emeralds, and rubies that fill every window and counter top.

Of course, midtown west's best-known attraction is the theatre district around Times Square. At the beginning of the twentieth century, this was the prime center of New York's social life. Charles Frohman established one of the first theatres in 1893 at 40th Street and Broadway, quickly followed by Oscar Hammerstein's Olympia a few blocks to the north. As more theatres opened, along came the lavish restaurants such as Rector's Café De L'Opera. In 1904, Adolph Ochs built his Times Tower adjoining one of the first subway stations in New York—named appropriately, Times Square. As movie houses became popular during the twenties and thirties, the theatres there gradually shuttled into side streets such as Shubert Alley. But the district remained intact and in fact grew synergistically as the media industry—newspapers, radio, publishing, film production, and later TV studios—all vied with one another for prime location. In the thirty-five-year period between 1930 and 1965, almost 80 million square feet of office space was erected in northern midtown west, the most notable complex, of course, being Rockefeller Center, built on a once-fashionable but deteriorating residential area.

Today, although the theatre district has degenerated somewhat in the southern portion around Times Square, it remains one of the most cohesive sectors in the city. The bars and taverns reflect, almost without exception, theatrical traditions. The legendary Sardi's (primarily a restaurant), Downey's, Artist and Writers, and Joe Allen still flourish, although there are several significant newcomers on the scene—Charlie's, Jimmy Ray's, Great Aunt Fanny's, Barrymore's and Ma Bell's. In the heart of the nearby media industry district, places like Jimmy's (only recently established, and amazingly popular) attract the stars of TV, film, and theatre. A little further to the west, around Eighth and Ninth avenues, places like Improvisation (impromptu theatrical cabaret and comedians), Jilly's (famous as Frank Sinatra's favorite New York watering hole), and the unusual Tripple Inn, provide a diversity of bar scene unmatched in the city. All that is missing is the 52nd Street scene that emerged as the major, if slightly risqué, nightlife center during prohibition. Scores of jazz clubs and speakeasies filled the strip's brownstone basements. It was, unfortunately, short-lived. Nothing remains today, except a handful of jazz bars including Jimmy Ryan's, all relocated on 54th Street.

THE ANGRY SQUIRE

ADDRESS: 216 Seventh Ave. (between 22nd and 23rd sts.);
242–9066
BAR HOURS: Noon–4 A.M.
FOOD: American/English (inexpensive)
CREDIT CARDS: None
DRESS: Very casual
SPECIAL FEATURES: Live jazz, darts tournaments on Tues.,
Sat. and Sun. brunch noon–4 P.M.
LIVELIEST TIMES: 10 P.M.–2 A.M. Tues.–Fri.

Frank Godin, a Liverpudlian who, until recently, owned another favorite Chelsea meeting place, Mr. Spatts, should be proud of the mellow, pub-like atmosphere of his Angry Squire. Following a disastrous fire in 1970 which closed the place for almost eight months, Mr. Godin and his manager, Kevin O'Doherty, re-created its warm intimacy. Beer barrels hang over the bar and fish nets loop between the roof beams and old lamps. Tall booths cluster along one of the walls; framed prints and old hand-colored maps of the British Isles glow in the candlelight.

In addition to being the local pub for such notable Chelsea-ites as Arthur Clarke and Arthur Miller, the Angry Squire has gained a considerable reputation for its English cuisine, which features shepherd's pie, fish 'n' chips (in real ale batter), steak and kidney pie, and sherry trifle. And if you're an English beer lover, there's Whitbread draft available at the bar.

When he first took over the place in 1969, Mr. Godin intended to let the kitchen develop slowly. However, it was not to be. On the first day, Gene Nelson brought in the whole cast of *Follies* and continued to fill the place for weeks until rehearsals were complete and the show moved uptown. "It was a bit of a bind," Mr. Godin said. "We only had a couple of pans and a spatula."

On another occasion, Halston, the famous designer, held a late-night party at the pub. Nine Rolls Royces, complete with uniformed chauffeurs, stood waiting outside. All went well until the early hours when the garbage trucks rolled up. The shimmering limousines were parked so close together that the garbage men

couldn't get to the sacks, cans, and boxes on the sidewalk with-out walking half a block in each direction. The chauffeurs re-fused to move, so the garbage men strolled bodily into the pub and told the sequinned and tuxedoed guests to get their %'!!$%! machines moved, or else! So nine disgruntled chauffeurs had to shift and shunt the great cars around while the smiling garbage men loaded their truck at a leisurely pace.

The Angry Squire is particularly noted for its jazz concerts held most evenings at 10 P.M. Weekends are the big-star nights with such occasional names as John Lewis, John Foster, and Dakota Staton. Needless to say, the place gets crowded. But if you're looking for a quiet niche, try the basement bar.

121

ARTISTS AND WRITERS RESTAURANT

ADDRESS: 213 W. 40th St. (at Seventh Ave.); LO 3–2424
BAR HOURS: Mon.–Fri. 11:30 A.M.–10:30 P.M. or midnight (depending on show times)
FOOD: American (moderate)
CREDIT CARDS: AE BA CB DC MC
DRESS: Semiformal
SPECIAL FEATURES: Atmosphere
LIVELIEST TIMES: Most evenings before and after theatre

Artists and Writers Restaurant has all the aura of a rather exclusive gentlemen's club, particularly in the rear dining room behind the long front bar, where tables are often reserved almost religiously for the regular daily patrons. Nevertheless, for all its apparent exclusive overtones, and dark-paneled decor, it's a most inviting place even for the uninitiated.

Over the past twenty years it has been owned by a pair of gentlemen referred to as Fitz and Hitz, although since the recent death of his partner, Mr. Hitz has been running it alone. Previously, it was known as Bleeck's—another rather sedate establishment once frequented by the staff of the old *Herald Tribune*. Although the same group still return occasionally for reunions, they find a more varied clientele of theatre people, sports stars and fans from the nearby Madison Square Garden, and workers from the garment district.

The atmosphere is generally quiet, but occasionally it becomes rather feverish in the afternoon when excitement centers around the match game tournaments held here. In fact, hanging on the wall is a series of original sketches by James Thurber depicting the ten steps in the match game.

Other fascinating artifacts—those curious bits and pieces of miscellania often found in taverns with long and established traditions—include a tarpon, caught off Block Island by J. P. Morgan and presented to Fitz and Hitz; a suit of armor that mysteriously disappeared from the prop room of the Metropolitan Opera Company; a copy of a prize-winning photograph of Babe Ruth at his retirement; and the number plate removed, again somewhat

mysteriously, from the last steam engine run by the Pennsylvania Railroad.

One last curious feature should be noted. At the back of the rear dining room is a small curtain. When performances are being held at the adjacent Billy Rose Theatre, the curtain is drawn back and the doors opened to admit both performers and audience to the Artist and Writers—one way of making a grand entrance on Broadway without ever having to memorize a line!

123

THE BRIEFKASE PUB

ADDRESS: Port Authority Bus Terminal (41st St. at Eighth Ave.)
2nd floor; 947-0439
BAR HOURS: 10 A.M.–11 P.M. Mon.–Sat., noon–11 P.M. *Sun.*
FOOD: None
CREDIT CARDS: None
DRESS: Informal
SPECIAL FEATURES: Sports museum, 97¢ martini up to 7 P.M.
LIVELIEST TIMES: Variable (due to location)

From its nondescript appearance, the Briefkase Pub looks like just another quick-drink-before-the-bus place. And many of its patrons see it as just that. But to a sports freak—the kind who gets excited by a baseball signed by Ty Cobb, Ted Williams, Rogers Hornsby, George Sisler, and Bill Terry or by the football from the 1934 Columbia-Stanford Rose Bowl Game—this place is paradise.

The Pub is named after the sports column writer in the old *Journal-American,* Max Kase, and is a truly amazing museum of sports memorabilia. Kase was actually the proprietor until his recent death, and many of the exhibits are part of his personal collection. Y. A. Tittle's helmet is here, along with the gloves worn by Joe Louis when he defeated Billy Conn in 1946. The actual ringside bell from the 1919 Dempsey-Willard fight is mounted on a wall next to an enlarged photo of the fight and a copy of the *New York Times* headlines the day after. Signed contracts for Joe DiMaggio, Yogi Berra, and Babe Ruth are all here, appropriately framed and appropriately admired. How about original Rube Goldberg cartoons? Or original cartoons by Willard Mullin, Bill Gallo, or Burris Jenkins, Jr.?

While most of this collection of memorabilia is at the pub on 41st St. and Eighth Ave., you might be able to see some living sports legends at the Briefkase Pub No. 2 across from Madison Square Garden on 33rd Street and Eighth Avenue—a strange little black and white cube, but particularly popular with Knicks and Rangers stars.

CHARLIE'S

ADDRESS: 263 W. 45th St. (between B'way and Eighth Ave.);
   354–2911
BAR HOURS: 11:30 A.M.–4:00 A.M.
FOOD: American (moderate)
CREDIT CARDS: AE BA MC
DRESS: Casual
SPECIAL FEATURES: Sunday brunch noon–5 P.M.
LIVELIEST TIMES: 6 P.M.–2 A.M. every evening

One of the regular patrons of Charlie's gave us his version of how this delightful place came to be. He's an actor and apparently he and many of his professional friends often look for somewhere to go after performances. Because of its familiarity, the first response to "Where shall we have a drink?" was "Not DOWNEY'S." In fact, he suggested that Charlie's be called "Not Downey's" since it was established as an alternative to that venerable, almost hallowed, enclave of theatrical tradition.

Judging from the popularity of Charlie's, however, they could have called it anything and it would have been a success. Not only does it offer that special clublike atmosphere so loved by theatrical performers, but owners Charles Dobson and Charles Harder brought with them an extensive experience and a strong friendship developed during their previous service at Joe Allen, where one was manager and the other head bartender. This place could also have been called "Not Joe Allen's" for much of the same crowd frequents both establishments.

Before the opening of Charlie's in June of 1973 this was the site of two old-time theatre spots: the Theatre Bar and the Showspot. The Charlies tore out the connecting wall and joined the two places. Now one side shelters the bar and a few tables and the other side is primarily for dining. Although there's no singles trade here, the bar is always packed, and because of this before- and after-theatre dining reservations are mandatory.

Our friend, the actor, points out that the popularity of the place is in great part due to the care and consideration shown

125

to regular customers by the two Charlies. If an actor is on the move he can have scripts sent here. Some members of the profession often spend hours over drinks at the tables, silently reading and rehearsing their parts—and no one would ever dream of disturbing them. So, if you'd like to see the place many performers call home, visit Charlie's. You'll feel as welcome as any star.

DOWNEY'S

ADDRESS: 705 Eighth Ave. (between 44th and 45th Sts.); PL
    7–0186
BAR HOURS: 11:30 A.M.–2 A.M.; closed Sun.
FOOD: American (expensive)
CREDIT CARDS: AE DC
DRESS: Semiformal
SPECIAL FEATURES: Photographs of Broadway stars, Irish coffee
LIVELIEST TIMES: 6 P.M.–8 P.M. and 10 P.M.–midnight each
    night

If Sardi's is a little too formal, yet you're determined to have a drink where people in the theatre traditionally go, then Downey's would be an ideal choice. Even if you don't happen to see the famous names of show business in the flesh, you can spend your time trying to name all the stars in the photographs that cover most of the walls in this pleasantly dignified establishment. But note: The photographs are strictly of Broadway stars. Movie stars who haven't appeared on Broadway, no matter how renowned, aren't featured, while many minor performers in Broadway productions are.

The photographs are true status symbols; when a new performer appears on Broadway, he invariably sends his agent over to Downey's requesting a session with their special photographer to provide him with a little instant immortality. These photos, which actually cost Downey's $75.00 each, are a major investment. When a fire broke out four years ago, one of the manager's main concerns was the water damage to his hundreds of treasured prints, many of which were, of course, irreplaceable. Ironically,

126

Downey's was not originally established as an enclave for theatre folk. Founder Jim Downey's prime interest was his race horses; his bar was more of a personal club for like-minded friends and gentlemen wagerers. (Brendan Behan provides a few fascinating insights of Jim in his book *Brendan Behan's New York*.) Inevitably, however, because of its location, Downey's attracted the knowns and unknowns of Broadway. Many of the struggling actors Jim Downey helped eventually became famous and continue to frequent the establishment along with their equally famous friends.

The place is full of stories and traditions, but the best way to understand Downey's is to go in for a smooth Irish coffee before or after the theatre. Don't be put off by the somewhat dubious reputation of the area; Downey's has and will continue to survive as long as Broadway has theatres and stars have egos.

GIORDANO'S

ADDRESS: 409 W. 39th St. (at Ninth Ave.); 947–9811
BAR HOURS: Mon.–Fri. noon–1:30 A.M., Sat. 5 P.M.–midnight,
   Sun. 2:30 P.M.–10:30 P.M.
FOOD: Italian and American (expensive—no menus)
CREDIT CARDS: AE BA CB DC MC
DRESS: Smart casual
SPECIAL FEATURES: Location!
LIVELIEST TIMES: 10 P.M.–1 A.M. Wed.–Sat.

Giordano's is in one of those hidden locations known mainly to those who live or work in the neighborhood. And what a neighborhood this is! Markets spill over the sidewalks, offering an almost surrealistic display of sheep's heads, tongues, sacks of spices, Italian breads, Filipino snacks, the finest prosciutto in New York, and a fascinating range of gnarled and pimpled vegetables.

Standing at the intersection of Ninth Avenue and 39th Street it's hard to imagine that hidden somewhere (probably behind a large cantaloupe) is a charming Italian restaurant and bar. However, close to the Port Authority parking lot, and almost the last door on the right, is a sign announcing Giordano's—a sign that has proclaimed the existence of this place for more than sixteen years.

When first established, Giordano's had four tables for dining. Now there are four separate dining rooms (including a converted stable) surrounding a central courtyard, in addition to a bar area and plans for a larger cocktail lounge with live entertainment. In place of the four original tables—where immigrants used to meet and play cards—is the kitchen which is also in the process of expansion.

Even though most of the people who lived in the area when Giordano's was founded have long since moved out, they still come back for the Italian cuisine and camaraderie. The Giordanos are especially proud of their food and stress that they do all their own butchering and make their own pasta.

But with the expanded cocktail lounge this should become a great haven for those to whom food is not a primary concern. Bruno Giordano plans to offer entertainment without a cover or minimum charge—so what better way to enjoy your chianti or to recover from the trauma of a market expedition in this area?

GREAT AUNT FANNY'S

ADDRESS: 340 W. 46th St. (between eighth and ninth aves.);
765–7374
BAR HOURS: Mon., Tues., Thurs., and Fri. 4 P.M.–2 A.M., Wed.
and Sat. noon–2 A.M., Sun. 1 P.M.–midnight
FOOD: American (moderate)
CREDIT CARDS: AE MC
DRESS: Casual
SPECIAL FEATURES: Cocktail hour 4 P.M.–6 P.M.
LIVELIEST TIMES: 10 P.M.–2 A.M. Wed.–Sat.

Whereas most people have an imaginary friend or villain in their youth, owner Bill Cressler had an imaginary guardian as an adult—Great Aunt Fanny. Great Aunt Fanny would take care of things and would zap you for something bad. So when it came time to name his new restaurant, it had to be Great Aunt Fanny's.

It's an elegant place where you can dress as casually or extravagantly as you wish; where people feel at home; where there is an atmosphere of friendship. For his friends in the theatre business, Bill felt this was exactly the kind of place they needed—and it appears he's right. Most dishes on the menu are named after friends or investors. There's Jane's apple nut cake (Jane Powell), potatoes Nelson (Gene Nelson), potatoes Mitchell (Chad Mitchell), etc. But because actors can be young and poor, as well as established, the menu includes everything from hamburgers on up. Two actors' specialties, inexpensive and delicious, include Choate salad (bacon, spinach, and mushrooms) and eggs Marlene (poached eggs, creamed spinach, and melted cheese). And Bill doesn't care what you order, as long as you're happy. In fact, to make you happy, he'll even suggest other places to try when Great Aunt Fanny's is too crowded.

The decor is casual yet elegant, with brick walls, crisp linen tablecloths, and an old baby grand piano. On Sunday, showcase auditions for show backers are held here. And during the week—with a little advance notice to Bill—local show people can come in and perform briefly (he doesn't want a cabaret atmosphere, so he discourages more than a few songs). There is a small intimate

130

bar at the front, plus an equally small drinking area next to it. Between the two are the Alexis Smith memorial steps; apparently the long-legged actress has tripped on them just often enough to brand them as her own.

JIMMY RAY'S

ADDRESS: 729 Eighth Ave. (between 45th and 46th Sts.); 582–9507

BAR HOURS: Noon–4 A.M., Sun. 4 P.M.–4 A.M.

FOOD: American (moderate)

CREDIT CARDS: None

DRESS: Very informal

LIVELIEST TIMES: 6P.M.–8P.M. and 10 P.M.–midnight most evenings

One thing you can say unequivocally for Jimmy Ray's: It certainly isn't one of those posh, sterile just-put-together places the theatre crowd likes to patronize. In fact, even though there's a heavy theatre following here, little has been done to encourage it.

There's no entertainment, no TV, very little lighting (so it's hard to be seen), one or two random photographs, and an overall musty feel.

Prior to being taken over by Jimmy Ray seven years ago, this was Gilhoolie's, an Irish pub of strange reputation. Women weren't allowed to sit at the bar or smoke anywhere in the pub. It was even mustier then too. Jimmy put in air conditioning, moved the kitchen upstairs, made a few improvements to the decor, and generally added a little finesse. But it still remains a rather unusual place, attracting a dual clientele. In the evening the theatre crowd dominates; but at other times the place is full of young, clean-cut regulars, most of whom know and enjoy one another's company.

One woman we talked to says she likes Jimmy Ray's because she can always find intelligent conversation here and added that there's another reason she spends a lot of time in the pub—the gas fire is always lit in the winter, and it's a terrific place to huddle when it gets cold!

LANDMARK TAVERN

ADDRESS: 46th St. (at Eleventh Ave.); 757–8595
BAR HOURS: Noon–1 A.M. daily
FOOD: American and Irish specials (moderate)
CREDIT CARDS: None
DRESS: Informal
SPECIAL FEATURES: Sun. brunch noon–5 P.M.
LIVELIEST TIMES: 9 P.M.–11 P.M. weekends

This is another O'Neal establishment, and it really shows how experience and good management can transform the unlikeliest of places. It was originally a longshoreman's bar established in 1868 and situated across the street from the present location. Inevitably it spanned prohibition as a speakeasy and was later moved to its current site. Now, following the O'Neal renovation, it's a delightful spot, attracting an interesting range of patrons, includ-

133

ing television and theatre celebrities, with its Victorian charm. However, the area with its warehouses and grimy streets provides a most unusual and unexpected contrast. Of course, there's method in the O'Neals' apparent madness. If all goes according to the city's plan there will soon be a huge convention center in the area that will doubtless revive the entire neighborhood. It's quiet—certainly not as rowdy as some of the places on nearby Restaurant Row—and offers separate dining and drinking areas.

Upstairs is an especially chintzy dining room, again with Victorian overtones, usually used for parties and banquets. Grandmother would have loved it!

MA BELL'S

ADDRESS: 218 45th St. (at Shubert Alley); 869–0110
BAR HOURS: Noon–midnight Mon.–Sat, closed Sun.
FOOD: American and European (moderate)
CREDIT CARDS: AE BA CB DC MC
DRESS: Semiformal
SPECIAL FEATURES: Old-fashioned phones on the tables, an eighty-foot bar, $2 minimum at the tables
LIVELIEST TIMES: Most evenings, before and after the theatre

Ma Bell's is misunderstood and will doubtless continue to create confusion until there's a name change. Many people actually come in here to pay their bills and find it hard to comprehend the presence of an eighty-foot bar lined with beer mugs and cocktail glasses. Their confusion is even further exacerbated by the phones on the tables and in the dining booths. They're the old-fashioned models, but they work and can be used for table-to-table calls or calls anywhere in the vicinity.

The walls of this rather unusual establishment are covered with poster-sized photographs of famous people—some with telephones, all with humorous captions. Humorous, that is, if they're poking fun at someone you think deserves it. For example, one man refused to be seated in a booth where Richard Nixon was subject to a facetious caption. Usually, however, patrons wait in line for that particular booth!

Because of its location in Shubert Alley, Ma Bell's gets a large but mature theatre-going crowd. There's rarely any blue jean trade here, although the place has an easy-going air and the bartenders, at least the ones we met, are some of the friendliest in the area and very quick with the wit.

135

R. J. SCOTTY'S

ADDRESS: 202 Ninth Ave. (between 22nd and 23rd sts.); 741–2148
BAR HOURS: Noon–midnight
FOOD: Italian (moderate)
CREDIT CARDS: None
DRESS: Informal
SPECIAL FEATURES: Cocktail hour 4 P.M.–5:30 P.M. Mon.–Friday, brunch Sat. and Sun.
LIVELIEST TIMES: 8 P.M.–10:30 P.M. Wed.–Fri.

Renato Lesizza, owner of R. J. Scotty's, used to own a number of restaurants including Original Mario's and the delightful BILLY-MUNK. But business was keeping him too busy, so he sold them all and moved into this one location, which he named R. J. Scotty's, after his two-year-old son.

The building is over seventy years old and the bar itself has a history almost as long, including the traditional speakeasy phase, when illicit goings-on were centered in the basement, traditionally equipped with buzzers and peepholes. When Renato moved in he had to overcome the previous bar's rather dubious reputation. For over six months he cleaned, remodeled, and refurbished the place and at times, almost had to drag patrons in off the street to prove that there was indeed a new owner and a new policy at the tavern.

Today Scotty's has a large front-bar area usually tended by charming barmaids, and at the rear there's an intimate dining room, ideal in atmosphere for the Italian cuisine prepared by Renato, who does all the cooking. His skill, particularly with sauces, has developed a strong neighborhood following in this part of Chelsea, in addition to a regular trade of local theatrical people and businessmen.

Scotty's is by no means a fancy place, and unlike many of the better-known Village taverns, there's plenty of room for relaxed, unhurried conversation. However, it has a special kind of charm all its own, the food has an unusually high reputation, and Renato deserves much credit for brightening up a rather dull stretch of Ninth Avenue.

THURSDAY'S

ADDRESS: 57 W. 58th St. (between Fifth and Sixth aves.); 371–7777
BAR HOURS: Sun.–Thurs. 11:45 A.M.–3 A.M., Fri.–Sat. 11:45 A.M.–4 A.M.
FOOD: American (expensive)
CREDIT CARDS: AE DC MC
DRESS: Casual
SPECIAL FEATURES: Cocktail hour 5 P.M.–8 P.M. (hot hors d'oeuvres), Sun. brunch 11:45 A.M.–4:30 P.M.
LIVELIEST TIMES: Cocktail hour and 10 A.M.–2 A.M. Tues.–Sun.

Don't skip this review because you think Thursday's is just like TUESDAY's, Wednesday's, or FRIDAY's. Owners Ben Benson, Alan Stillman, and Ernie Kalman have made a conscious effort to ensure that each has its own unique identity and following. For example, this is not a place for swinging singles, although there are some singles at the bar in the evening. Mostly, however, it's a place for couples, twenty-five and over, to enjoy drinks or dinner. Also, this is not a discotheque, although there is a small dance floor suspended between two dining levels. But even if you're dining or drinking near the dance floor, you're barely aware of it because of its size and location—and the establishment is so vast that you can get away from it entirely if you prefer.

But don't let the size of Thursday's put you off. It's beautifully divided into many separate areas, all a few steps up or down from each other, and all distinct. There are two bar and cocktail lounge areas. One of the bars, left over from the former Escadrille private club—is like a tri-wing plane with a brass ceiling, brass bar top, and brass wing at the bottom. The largest dining area (and you may drink here anytime) is designed as a garden, with dozens of lovely trees growing in pots and fresh flowers on the tables. In fact, it costs the management about $1,000 a week just to keep the greenery green. This same area is also decorated with antique mirrors and lamps, all different, and all proud discoveries of Ben

137

Benson. It's a true delight, the food is varied, the service is excellent, and the menu is hilarious if you read it slowly.

Special drinks of the house include a piña colada, rich with pineapple and coconut, and a Sock-it-to-me Strawberry that has to be the best treat in town on a warm day. For many people, Thursday's will come as a surprise, and a pleasant one. On the west side, it is unique, yet is often skipped by those who would enjoy it. Take our word for it, and find out for yourself that Thursday's is not just like any other day of the week.

WEST BOONDOCK

ADDRESS: 114 Tenth Ave. (at 17th St.); 929–9645
BAR HOURS: Noon–2 A.M. Mon.–Thurs., noon–4 A.M. Fri., 5 P.M.–
   3 A.M. Sat. and Sun.
FOOD: Soul food and American (inexpensive)
CREDIT CARDS: AE CB DC MC
DRESS: Casual
SPECIAL FEATURES: Jazz nightly from 8 P.M.
LIVELIEST TIMES: 8 P.M. onwards most evenings

When West Boondock opened nine years ago, it was looked upon as a strange place in an even stranger location. The location, down by the decaying Hudson River docks, is still a bit odd, but the West Boondock has now become a truly entrenched and established part of the Manhattan jazz bar scene.

The initial skepticism is understandable. This was the first place to commercially offer soul food outside Harlem. It also encouraged a racially integrated clientele and offered good jazz with no cover charge or drink minimum. And over the years owner Victor Gaston, Sr., has retained these policies. The only thing he'd really like to change is the size of the place, but since it's impossible to enlarge, customers waiting for seats will continue to jam the entrance of this small club. It used to be an Irish saloon and is still set up for that kind of business, with the long bar taking up almost half of the space. The piano for the jazz duos

that play on different nights of the week seems almost incidental in its location at the end of the room. All the walls and the ceilings are painted black, and the gold balls hanging on strings from the rafters give the impression of a deep sea view of an oceanic mine field. Screen curtains of a red and black print based on an African drum decoration block out almost all incoming light. The whole dark, introverted mood is extremely conducive to the fine jazz played here.

Mr. Gaston feels the unexpected success of West Boondock inspired many of the recent facilities now offering soul food—including the black-eyed peas currently sold through the Horn and Hardart vending machines. But he still has no real competition in the area. People come from all over for the food and music, and with no cover, the bar is also packed nightly.

While the crowd here is young, twenty-five through forty, it's a mature, sophisticated group. During the day his clientele includes people from the Wall Street area, film studio personnel, truck drivers, executives, and nearby waterfront workers. Occasionally celebrities, such as Lena Horne or Barbra Streisand, stop by.

In Chelsea the mood changes block by block. West Boondock seems to have taken the best of all moods, mixed them up, and brought in some outside influences. The result is a winning combination of good food, good music, and interesting people.

and for your further enjoyment...

BARRYMORE'S

ADDRESS: 267 W. 45th St. (between Broadway and Eighth Ave.);
   541-4500

Since there are only a handful of worthwhile drinking spots in
the theatre district, any new establishment of quality is welcome.
And while the people in this area are still discovering the recently
opened Barrymore's, patrons are already coming from the local
garment district, advertising companies, film labs, television net-
works, and the theatre to what used to be the Showcase Bar. It
is starting out with a more informal atmosphere than many of
the other neighboring spots, and the moderately priced menu
attracts those with a smaller budget. It's also less crowded than
the most established places, so it's a better place to relax. If it
can maintain this casual pace, we are sure it will do well in an
area that needs as much variety in its bars as it does in its shows.

THE ENGLISH PUB

900 Seventh Ave. (between 56th and 57th sts.); 265-4360

The late-night scene is rather pathetic in this part of Manhattan. Or at least it was until 1973, when Arnold Stein opened
his English Pub as a haven for the after-theatre crowd, pilots
and stewardesses from nearby hotels, and even barmen from
other local taverns that close around midnight. Four A.M. invariably comes too soon for this lively crowd.

As one might expect, decor is a little too "English"—there are
at least six stags' heads, the place is littered with London street
signs, Union Jacks abound (even on the menus), and the half-
timbered walls have a kind of Hollywood look. However, for all
this, it's a warm, friendly place, cocktail hour hors d'oeuvres are
excellent, drinks are generous (especially the sours), and it's just
what the area needed.

141

IMPROVISATION

384 W. 44th St. (at Ninth Ave.); 765–8268

A tiny gem of a place in a somewhat unlikely location. At minimal cost ($3–$5) seekers of the unusual can enjoy mini-revues by talented off-Broadway actors and occasional impromptu appearances of some of Broadway's finest stars in this murky, theatrical-decor tavern. It's a late-scene place—busy from 9:30 most evenings—but it's always changing, and you never know what's going to happen next. Give them a call before setting off for the wilds of Ninth Avenue.

JILLY'S

256 W. 52nd St. (at Eighth Ave.); 581–5564

Sinatra-lovers will know this place well. Jilly Rizzo and Old Blue-Eyes have been close friends for many years, and whenever the original superstar appears in Manhattan concerts Jilly is always close by in the wings or sitting on the stage steps.

Afterwards, at Jilly's bar-restaurant, it's invariably a mob scene, but only a very few (hundred!) get to stay after 4 A.M. when Sinatra, backed by his pianist, may croon a few of his oldies.

When Francis Albert is away, Jilly's is just another pleasant cocktail lounge located in a quaint old building on the fringe of the theatre district. There's usually a jazz trio in the background and the menu contains an unusual selection of steaks and Chinese dishes.

JIMMY RYAN'S

154 W. 54th Ct. (between Sixth and Seventh aves.); CO 5–9505

In the mid-thirties, 52nd Street was the jazz center of the world. Literally scores of clubs filled the cramped basements of old brownstones along Swing Street, featuring most of the popular notables of the era–Billie Holliday, Eddie Condon, Count Basie, Billy Daniels, and Nat "King" Cole. Inevitably, in the city of ever-changing tastes and cultures, the scene was short-lived. By the late fifties, the strip was dead and for a few years, jazz almost disappeared in Manhattan.

Today, fortunately, there's been a noted revival. The Village, Chelsea, and the upper west side now possess a number of popular jazz bands and Swing Street has even experienced a mini-revival on 54th Street with Jimmy Ryan's, Eddie Condon's Club, and the Half Note (recently closed, but possibly reopening).

Ryan's is a long, narrow basement establishment that offers, without cover or minimum, lively New Orleans jazz every evening. The renowned Roy Eldridge has been the prime attraction for more than five years, backed by Dick Katz (piano), Eddie Locke (drums), Major Holley (bass), and Bobby Pratt (trombone). Just one note for Eldridge-lovers. He often tends to appear late in the evening but he's worth waiting for, even if the drinks are a little expensive.

JOE ALLEN

326 W. 46th St. (between Eighth and Ninth aves.); 581–6464

Although the Joe Allen Restaurant and Tavern is almost too much of a Broadway tradition to mention, a drink or dinner here prior to or following theatre is one of those New York delights not to be missed.

143

Everyone comes to this cozy little place, snuggled in a Restaurant Row basement—celebrities, actors, society snobs, jet setters, students, tourists. It provides a visual cross section of Manhattan's amazingly diverse population, yet everyone is treated by the waiters with the same studied and slightly disinterested courtesy.

While decor lacks the suavity of other renowned theatre restaurants—Sardi's, Del Sommas, Spindletop—the brick walls covered in old photographs and posters, the wooden floor, the red-check tablecloths, provide a delightful atmosphere of casual intimacy. It's a lovely place, thick with theatre tradition.

THE TRIPPLE INN

263 W. 54th St. (between Broadway and Eighth Ave.); CI 5–9849

Don't be put off by the rather somber appearance of this small pub (at its previous location on Eighth Avenue, patrons were required to press a buzzer and be recognized before entering!). It's an extremely lively place during the late evening (10 P.M.–2 A.M.) and attracts a mixed clientele of actors, theatre-goers, and policemen from the 18th Precinct across the street.

In addition to being a Knickerbocker Darts League pub with its own female team, the Sex-o-Lets, the Tripple Inn offers a showcase on Wednesdays and often hilarious open-house cabarets on Thursdays, Fridays, and Saturdays.

Decor is familiar—sawdust, beer pitchers, assorted dangling bric-a-brac—but the flavor is unique in this part of town.

MIDTOWN EAST

Once referred to as "The Nerve Center of the Lunch Counter" or alternatively, "The Genteel Jungle," midtown east is the heart of Manhattan's high service industries—advertising, publishing, movies, photography, journalism, decorating, designing—and politicking! Its contrasting environment of brownstone streets, towering steel and glass offices, remodelled mews carriage houses (Sniffen Court in the Murray Hill area is an outstanding example) and the great Grand Central Station complex, is a far cry from the late eighteenth century when much of the area consisted of small rural estates. It was on the Murray Estate, later to become an area of fashionable town houses, that Mrs. Robert Murray served afternoon tea to prominent British officers while her companions assisted the escape of revolutionary soldiers during the War of Independence. In the mid-1800s Murray Hill, as it was later known, became the home of many of Mrs. Astor's famous "400" guests and the setting for Edith Wharton's novels. It was described by one historian as "a patch of residential elegance" and remained largely that way until the mid-twentieth century, when an 1847 ordinance restricting businesses in the area was repealed.

Murray Hill and the elite residences along Fifth Avenue were exceptional enclaves in an area of "brown houses, smoking chimneys and manure-filled streets, remarkable for its drabness and lack of distinction." Also, further to the east along the river, lay Turtle Bay, a notorious area of tenements, slaughterhouses, glue factories, and the vilest collection of noxious industries in the city. There were few relieving features here except perhaps the Turtle Bay Gardens, a delightful town house complex remodelled in 1920 to create a central interior garden, and the Tudor City Apartments erected in 1928. Understandably, both developments were based on an inward-facing design. Not one window of the Tudor City complex overlooked Turtle Bay. Unfortunately, no

145

provision was made for later modification when the United Nations complex eradicated the whole of the Turtle Bay mess, stimulated the improvement of nearby brownstones into the now-fashionable Beekman and Sutton places, and opened up some of the most striking river views in the city!

As with the Gramercy district, one of the area's primary spines is Third Avenue. During the old days it was a dismal Irish slum, but when the overhead tracks were removed in 1955, the avenue experienced a rapid renaissance. Fortunately, its Irish flavor remained, and today it still possesses some of the finest old and new Irish pubs in the city, including Costello's, the John Barleycorn, Brew's and P. J. Clarke's. And the Anglo-Irish flavor is by no means limited to Third Avenue. In fact, throughout the neighborhood can be found a score or more splendid taverns such as Billymunk, Duncan's, the Green Derby, the Three Farthings, the Green Man, Charlie Brown's, the Guardsman, David Copperfield's, Desmond's, and O'Caseys.

Inevitably the midtown area, because of its commercial character suffers to some extent from the downtown syndrome. Many pubs do a roaring lunch and cocktail-hour trade and then close early after the commuters have finally staggered out through the doors. However, the following reviews relate primarily to bars that manage to attract a healthy evening trade and include a few that are remarkable for their evening popularity, particularly with the younger crowd—Rumm's, Peartrees, Goose and Gherkin, the Green Derby, Brew's and the John Barleycorn. Ironically, many of these places also draw a large contingent from the Wall Street area who leave the downtown pubs after cocktail hour to join the swinging set a little further uptown.

Other places boast a hearty night scene by virtue of live entertainment—O'Lunneys, Michael's Pub, Dionysus, the Blue Angel. Then there are the older more traditional establishments such as Costello's, P. J. Clarke's and the Reidy's which never seem to change—they just become more and more popular. It's a fascinating tavern scene in midtown east, and one that is too often underestimated by Manhattan residents. Explore and enjoy.

BILLYMUNK

ADDRESS: 302 E. 45th St. (at Second Ave.); 684–0973
BAR HOURS: 11:30 A.M.–4 A.M.
CREDIT CARDS: AE BA CB DC MC
FOOD: American/Irish (moderate)
DRESS: Casual
SPECIAL FEATURES: Sun. brunch noon–5 P.M., off-Broadway theatre
  on the second floor, the "Kelly's Kick" cocktail
LIVELIEST TIMES: 9 P.M.–2 A.M. Wed.–Fri.

For connoisseurs of Cockney slang, otherwise referred to as rhyme slang, *billymunk* means drunk. If you don't know what we're talking about, read the framed newspaper clip by the door that explains all.

It's a great place, but until owner Pat Cooney painted the outside a garish red, with highlighted white moldings, it remained one of those obscure gems of Second Avenue. The building is over 120 years old and boasts a mottled history as a butcher's shop (when the UN site was a slaughterhouse), an Italian restaurant (Colombo's), a speakeasy, and finally a fine Irish-flavored watering hole complete with Guinness/Harp/Bass draft ales and an Irish-biased menu. Walk through to the very back (it's a long walk) and notice the 3,501 chianti bottles that form a ceiling for the rear room. Even better, look for the tiny niche to the left of the kitchen that encloses a couple of tables. There's a tiny section of the old speakeasy wall complete with caricatures of customers à la Palm's Restaurant (just down Second Avenue).

Billymunk offers mild relief (if that's what you want) from the midtown singles scene—otherwise known as the "bouncing track"—and that includes many of the local Irish taverns. One tends to find an Italian/Irish and otherwise mixed crowd of neighborhood locals attracted by the convivial spirit and an authentic atmosphere of old Manhattan—note the lithographs and photographs of old New York politicians. In addition, there's a recently established off-Broadway theatre/cabaret upstairs—well worth a visit.

Owners Pat and Moss Cooney are involved in a number of taverns around town, including O'CASEYS, MUNK'S PARK (a new location for the Village Bells of Hell crowd complete with Monday night Irish folksong session), and COONEYS.

Costello's

COSTELLO'S

ADDRESS: 225 E. 44th St. (near Third Ave.); 682–9713
BAR HOUSES: 8 A.M.–4 A.M. Mon.–Sat.; closed Sun.
FOOD: Irish/American (moderate)
CREDIT CARDS: AE DC
DRESS: Mixed
SPECIAL FEATURES: Thurber's "wall" sketches
LIVELIEST TIMES: 5 P.M.–8 P.M. most evenings

The true test of any bar's popularity comes when it is forced to leave the location in which it has become known and move to new headquarters. Costello's recently passed with flying colors. Not only did its old clientele follow the bar from its Third Avenue spot to its current location, but many new faces started to appear.

Part of the reason for this easy transition is that Tim Costello and Tom and Eddie Fitzpatrick, Costello's current owners, tried to bring as much of the old tavern with them as was literally possible. The hardest part of this task was moving the sketches done directly on the walls by James Thurber during the depression.

149

Fortunately most of the sketches were preserved and today are framed and hung on the walls at the new Costello's. Also, while they left the famous 9-inch thick layers of dust and cobwebs on the twenty-foot high ceiling at the old location, they relocated the original bar and back-bar intact.

The old hats hung on the back bar include Al Smith's and those of many famous old newspaper columnists whose papers have long since folded. You'll also see Ernest Hemingway's shillelagh, which he once broke over his head in true machismo style, having been challenged to perform the feat by John O'Hara. The remnants remain on the back bar, in perpetuity.

The large part of the current crowd at Costello's consists of British and Australian newspapermen who work locally in their newspapers' offices; and a hearty contingent from the *Daily News*. After speaking to one Australian journalist, we discovered the reason they call Costello's home is due to its never-flagging, never-changing Irish hospitality. There's always room for them at the crowded bar, and bartenders not only know what they drink, but pour it to each one's individual capacity.

Costello's clientele is primarily male, although females are no longer asked to leave the bar. However, Marilyn Monroe once sat down at the bar, and after she was told there was no orange juice for the screwdriver she requested nor any lime for the gin and tonic, stormed out in disgust, leaving behind a few juicy quotations on Costello's chauvinists.

Costello's always seems to welcome you. It's a heavy drinking-pub, although there's a good selection of Irish and American dishes (often served by Herbie, voted the "world's worst waiter" by the staff of *The Star*). If you want to test your drinking stamina, stop in Costello's and try an Irish martini—made with County Cork dry gin. There's a limit of three to a customer and, considering some of the customers they have, that's saying a lot about the strength of the drink.

DIONYSOS

ADDRESS: 304 E. 48th St. (at Second Ave.); 758–8240
BAR HOURS: 5 P.M.–4 A.M.; closed Sun.
FOOD: Greek/European/American (expensive)
CREDIT CARDS: AE CB DC MC
DRESS: Smart
SPECIAL FEATURES: Cabaret, dancing
LIVELIEST TIMES: Most evenings from 9 P.M.

Paul Sapounakis is a remarkable gentleman. Not only does he own Dionysos (with two partners) and the Blue Angel—two of the most popular cabaret-nightspots in town—but he's also a well-known architect/developer, interior designer, and show-producer. "I like to do things a little differently, and sometimes it works," was his modest explanation of the success of his two most unusual Manhattan establishments—unusual due to the fact that they are places where bar patrons can enjoy a whole evening's live entertainment without cover or minimum. Of course, in both instances, there are also elaborate, stage-side dining areas where guests can pay equally elaborate prices for ringside seats, but that's the whole secret. Paul offers an honest choice; and even at the tables, guests invariably feel they receive excellent value for their money. There's no penny-pinching with the cabarets, especially at the Blue Angel (123 East 54th between Park and Lexington avenues) which offers a ninety-minute Las Vegas-styled show —a take-off based on the film *Cabaret* coupled with outstanding vignettes of old-time movie stars and show-business celebrities. The bar here is housed in a glass booth overlooking the stage, and although the vantage point is excellent, most patrons seem to be more interested in entertaining themselves with that special vivacity unique to an intense singles crowd.

In contrast, Dionysos is a delightful Greek-styled tavern complete with white plaster walls, brightly cushioned booths, and a bar encrusted with hand-painted Middle Eastern tiles. The total effect is a dazzling and sensual environment ideal for the mature singles crowd that gathers here nightly.

There are two Greek shows during the evening, and bar patrons may view them from the bar area. However, if they want to see the shows up close, they must become dinner patrons, with a $2.50 per head music charge and a dinner tab for two that could easily run to $40.

After each dinner show there is a discotheque hour, and those at the bar may climb the few steps to the restaurant and dance to the live music. And everybody dances. Celebrities dance with admirers, waiters dance with patrons, and patrons dance in the aisles with each other. Girls come out of the audience to perform Greek dances and are usually rewarded with a shower of dollar bills.

It's a dramatic setting at all levels—from the sunken bar area to the tri-level dining area—and patrons invariably leave with beaming smiles, beads of perspiration, and lighter pocketbooks!

DUNCAN'S

ADDRESS: 303 E. 53rd St. (at Second Ave.); 838–6154
BAR HOURS: 11:30 A.M.–4 A.M.; closed Sun.
FOOD: American (moderate)
CREDIT CARDS: AE CB DC MC
DRESS: Semiformal
SPECIAL FEATURES: Piano bar, cocktail hour (5 P.M.–7 P.M. with hors d'oeuvres)
LIVELIEST TIMES: 6 P.M.–2 A.M. Wed.–Fri.

Don't be misled by the narrow street frontage and cramped doorway of Duncan's. Come on in and make yourself at home in the long, large establishment famed for its clientele of airline stewardesses, big names in the sporting business, and for its steaks.

As with many places in this neighborhood, dress requirements tend to be a little strict, but don't let that put you off. It's really a very warm bar-restaurant. Of course with a maitre d' like the diminutive John Henderson it's understandable. His dour looks and thick Scottish accent are misleading; his humor races as fast as some of the Mets and Ranger stars who visit the bar regularly, much to the delight of the patrons.

The decor has a kind of Irish flavor but most noticeable are the large lithographs of sporting scenes by Leroy Neiman—in fact it's a regular art gallery and very tasteful.

The singles scene predominates during the weeknights starting around cocktail hour. Wednesday nights, particularly when the big games are shown via cable, are often frantic. So if you're looking for a quieter time, pop in on a Saturday when the whole neighborhood seems to take a rest.

While you're in the area, have a look at Desmond's across the avenue. It's a less elaborate Irish-flavored place but attracts a lively mixed crowd. The brogue, beer, and blarney flow freely until the early hours, with live Irish music most evenings to fill in the quiet gaps.

FIRESIDE CAFE

ADDRESS: 523 Third Ave. (at 35th St.); MU 5–3826
BAR HOURS: 8 A.M.–4 A.M.
FOOD: American (inexpensive)
CREDIT CARDS: None
DRESS: Casual
LIVELIEST TIMES: Weekends 8 P.M.–2 A.M.

Here's a no-frills, no-gimmicks, no-singles establishment—a true neighborhood tavern for an older, predominantly Irish and German clientele. The owner, Mike McSherry, has a number of places around town all catering to their own loyal groups of regulars. It's perhaps not the kind of bar you'd think of visiting for a wild night on the town (although Friday's Talent Nights are often lively in the extreme), but it reflects much of the neighborhood character and flavor. Drinks are generous, and the food, which often includes such traditional dishes as corned beef and cabbage, Irish stew, and sliced London broil, is well-prepared and inexpensive.

If you're around the area on St. Patrick's Day, this is one of the places you shouldn't miss. Finbar, a seven-foot tall giant of a policeman, and his Emerald Society Irish Pipes Band, somehow cram themselves into the rear of the bar and raise the rafters with their lung-bursting music. The rest of the year always seems a little dull in comparison.

GOOSE AND GHERKIN

ADDRESS: 251 E. 50th St. (at Third Ave.); 371–4636
BAR HOURS: 11:30 A.M.–4 P.M. Mon.–Fri., 5 P.M.–4 A.M. Sat.
and Sun.
FOOD: American (moderate)
CREDIT CARDS: AE BA CB DC MC
DRESS: Very casual
SPECIAL FEATURES: Happy Hour 4 P.M.–7 P.M. with hors
d'oeuvres, occasional live jazz on Mon.
LIVELIEST TIMES: 5 P.M.–8 P.M. and 10 P.M.–2 A.M. Tue.–Fri.

There is nothing more delightful than to walk into a place that
beckons you from the outside and find it even more enticing on
the inside. That's the way it is at the Goose and Gherkin. Once
you step down the stairs, you are charmed by this bright, inviting drinking spot. If you walk past the friendly bar in front, you

will encounter a sunken dining room with a large windcw at the rear overlooking an appealing garden with waterfall. It's easy to picture yourself sharing a drink with a friend and whiling away time in this spacious room. But if you're alone, the bar is the place to sit. Owner David Picenso tries to meet every individual who comes in alone, and makes a special effort to make strangers feel at home.

He only recently took over full ownership of the place, and after diligent cleaning and brightening has the basis for a fine, friendly neighborhood spot. Even though there is a large crowd, he prides himself on the fact that the Goose and Gherkin is not cliquish.

But then the neighborhood of the Goose and Gherkin is not a run-of-the-mill neighborhood. On either side of this cozy spot are Lutèce and the Leopard, two of the most elegant and expensive restaurants in Manhattan. People often stop in here expecting it to be the same, and are usually pleasantly surprised to find it's not. One man, however, came in and asked if it were indeed Lutèce that he had just walked into. This was pre-renovation time and when he was told no, it wasn't, he replied: "No, you're right. It's more like grotesque."

David Picenso can look back on this and laugh now, because the place has changed so much since then. And he is in the process of continuing those changes. We wish him luck, and if we must further entice you inside, we'll add one minor aside: The place is staffed almost totally by actresses and models. Ordinarily, we might not even mention this, but since many people may remember Goose and Gherkin as it once was, and don't know it as it is today, we'll bait the hook a little.

THE GREEN DERBY

ADDRESS: 978 Second Ave. (at 52nd St.); 688–1250
BAR HOURS: 11:30 A.M.–4 P.M.
CREDIT CARDS: AE
FOOD: American/Irish (moderate)
DRESS: Casual
SPECIAL FEATURES: "Irish Night"—every Wed. free "Irish" drinks 7 P.M.–8 P.M., special cocktails
LIVELIEST TIMES: 6 P.M.–midnight Wed.–Fri.

Here's the first of the Jerry Toner and Terry O'Neill places (others include the JOHN BARLEYCORN, DESMOND'S, FLANAGAN'S, ABBEY TAVERN, BARRYMORE'S, and a second Green Derby at 45th Street and Lexington Avenue).

It's a strong singles pub with all the Irish trimmings: flags, a barman who speaks Gaelic as well as English, old maps and photographs, colleen waitresses, and a menu full of authentic "old country" dishes—Irish stew, steak and kidney pie, etc.

Somehow, even though the formula has been imitated a score or more times in the neighborhood, the Green Derby has a special spirit all its own (an innocent pun—for indeed spirits have been used to create a few unique and unusual cocktails here). While we can't particularly recommend it, many of the younger regulars seem to enjoy the Sloe Comfort Screw (driver) consisting of a lethal mixture of sloe gin, Southern Comfort, vodka, and orange juice. Of course it's the kind of drink one tends to order for somebody else—if the evening looks promising.

Wednesday Irish Nights are particularly active between 7 P.M. and 8 P.M. when customers can wallow in a torrent of free drinks —Irish coffee, Black Velvet (Guinness and champagne), and Cold Duck. Alternatively the nightly 4 P.M.–7 P.M. cocktail hour offers a generous variety of hot and cold hors d'oeuvres to the homeward-bound office crowd.

For all its blarney, the Green Derby has a strong celebrity following that includes Jimmy Breslin, Tommy Makem (of the Clancy Brothers), the Irish Rovers, and even occasional appear-

157

ances by Bernadette Devlin. It's a bubbly, fun place, and the crowd has plenty of life.

By the way, if you leave a little high on those strange cocktails and could swear the *N* on the sign outside is backwards, don't worry. It is!

THE GREEN MAN

ADDRESS: 133 E. 56th St. (at Lexington Ave.); 355-9014
BAR HOURS: Noon–midnight
FOOD: British and sandwiches (inexpensive)
CREDIT CARDS: AE BA CB DC MC
DRESS: Casual
SPECIAL FEATURES: Piano (6 P.M.–midnight) most evenings, cocktail hour 5 P.M.–8 P.M.
LIVELIEST TIMES: 5:30 P.M.–8 P.M. most evenings

How does one begin to describe this unusual little pub? For a start, it's one of the smallest places we've found in Manhattan, and if you're walking at a fast pace down 56th Street you'll miss it. Also, if you're looking for fancy signs you'll never find it. On the other hand, if you pause at the corner of Lexington Avenue and 56th Street and listen carefully, you'll hear the clarion calls of the Green Man echoing down the street: "Pint o' bitter, John," "Hello, luv," "How yer doin', lad?" A little bastion of Britain.

Owner Larry Carnell and bartender John Healy are a great English duo who relish the push, shove, and smoke of their authentic pub. There are few places in New York where you can find British Whitbread beer on tap—and there are even fewer places where the company is so lively and convivial. If you want to see the place in full swing come any night of the week during the 5 P.M.–8 P.M. cocktail hour when hot hors d'oeuvres are served at the back table. Alternatively, if you prefer a more tranquil atmosphere or a quiet game of darts downstairs in the basement room, pop in after 9 P.M. most evenings.

Larry Carnell opened the place two years ago and brought to

it many years of experience as a bartender, starting when he was thirteen years old in England and more recently at the Purple Onion in San Francisco and Molly Mogg's in Manhattan. He's an excellent raconteur—start by asking him where the name Green Man comes from.

Decor is a true miscellany—paintings, prints, British beer signs, old photographs. The great thing here is that there's no design—it just happened. Lovers of British pubs will know what we mean. Give it a try.

THE GUARDSMAN

ADDRESS: 243 Lexington Ave. (at 34th St.); MU 4–8275
BAR HOURS: 11:30 A.M.–4 A.M.
FOOD: Hamburgers with pita bread (inexpensive)
CREDIT CARDS: AE
DRESS: Casual
SPECIAL FEATURES: Folk singing 8 P.M.–1 A.M. Sat. and Sun.,
    darts and backgammon competitions

This is an unusual little place—and we love it. A couple of years ago it was virtually unknown except to a few loyal regulars. But thanks to the innovations of owner Ed Gormley and his managers, Hawk Norton and Bob Coffey, it's gained a strong, and very mixed, following.

Even the door handle, made from an old army sword, should indicate that there's nothing "usual" about this place. It boasts its own darts team (the Guardsman was the first place in Manhattan to have a dartboard—twenty-five years ago!), a backgammon contest every Sunday afternoon, a menu consisting primarily of hamburgers on pita bread, and a phone booth painted in red stripes to resemble a sentry box (actually brought from Ed's original uptown bar of the same name). And that's not all. In the back, near the darts room, is a library on either side of a baronial fireplace, and over the back-bar is a superb piece of contemporary stained glass by French artist Robert Pinard—its title, "Blue Boar with Glass," may be meaningful if you can push your way through the bar-huggers to get a good look at it.

159

Ed Gormley himself—artist, writer, carpenter, raconteur, and one-time member of the French liberation army—is as fascinating as his unusual pub. His love of American history is such that he used to dress himself, and often his staff, in appropriate period outfits and deliver descriptive monologues on Revolutionary and Civil War battles. Even today on every September 16 he gives his account of the British Murray Hill landing to an audience of enthralled (or occasionally startled) customers. The dining room setting is perfect for the occasion—dark panelled walls, Ogden prints of American military uniforms and events, and scores of regimental badges displayed in gilt-edged frames.

But Ed's interests are varied. At the time of our visits he was involved in plans for renovating the Guardsman, deciding on his next folk singer (Sat. and Sun. 8 P.M.–1 A.M.), and selecting a publisher for his next book . . . .

THE JOHN BARLEYCORN

ADDRESS: 209 E. 45th St. (off Third Ave.); YU 6–1088
BAR HOURS: 11:30 A.M.–4 A.M. Mon.–Fri., 5 P.M.–4 A.M. Sat.,
  5 P.M.–3 A.M. Sun.
FOOD: American (inexpensive)
CREDIT CARDS: AE CB DC
DRESS: Informal
SPECIAL FEATURES: Live Irish music 9 P.M.–2 A.M. every evening
LIVELIEST TIMES: 6 P.M.–2 A.M. every evening

This is one of seven Irish-flavored establishments in the city (plus a John Barleycorn Hotel in County Cork, Ireland) owned by two ex-stewards of the *Queen Mary*, Jerry Toner and Terry O'Neill. Day-manager at Barleycorn's on East 45th Street, Charles Cartwright, was also with Jerry and Terry on the *Queen Mary*. He claims that the two talented entrepreneurs have finally made Irish pubs respectable again in New York. Unfortunately this particular place doesn't have Guinness on tap, but makes up for it by featuring Irish (type) bacon, sausage, and "black pudding" on its brunch and dinner menus.

Irish folk music is a big attraction here and the big names in the business, Tommy Makem and the Irish Rovers, have had live albums recorded in the upstairs Bunratty Room—a miniature version of a baronial dining hall decked out with fine prints of Irish landscapes.

While Friday nights seem to attract the singles, for most of the week the place has a mixed clientele intent on enjoying good food, good beer—and usually, good music.

161

KITTY HAWK'S

ADDRESS: 565 Third Ave. (at 37th St.); 661–7406
BAR HOURS: Noon–4 A.M.
FOOD: American (moderate)
CREDIT CARDS: AE BA CB DC MC
DRESS: Casual
SPECIAL FEATURES: Brunch Sat. and Sun. and 11 P.M.–4 A.M.
    nightly
LIVELIEST TIMES: 10 P.M.–3 A.M. Wed.–Fri.

Here's yet another creation by Alan Stillman and Ben Benson of TUESDAY'S, Wednesday's, THURSDAY'S, and FRIDAY'S fame. The outside window displays a permanent photographic exhibition of early flying pioneers, men and women, standing beside their canvas and plywood machines, smiling with gusto and confidence. Inside it's unusually dark, even for New York bars, but once your eyes become accustomed to the gloom you'll notice the wealth of areonautical and other miscellanea that fills the place—a couple of superb wooden propellers, models of old planes, a section of tail and a battered wing-tip gas tank, a pilot's head-gear used as a lampshade. If that isn't enough there's an old tuba dangling from the ceiling, stuffed canaries in cages, a life belt, and even a baby's bathtub! The whole place feels like a Hemingway-influenced version of a World War I pilots' mess. Even the menus in the rear dining area are designed as flight plan documents, and many of the chairs are 1920s-styled wicker affairs —superb for lazy lounging over long cocktails.

Kitty Hawk's has developed a strong following among stewardesses who, according to management policy, always get their first drink free of charge. And of course where there are stewardesses there's normally a strong singles scene, although the crowd tends to be more mixed and more adult here, in contrast to the cruising places in the 60s and 70s.

One notable feature at Kitty Hawk's is the brunch, which is truly a gourmands delight, featuring a vast platter of ham, three eggs, stuffed French toast, muffins, etc., and all the champagne or

Bloody Mary's you can manage for a ridiculously low price. In fact, it's become so popular that it's available not only on weekends but also every single night of the week (11 P.M.–4 A.M.). However, a word of warning: The Sunday brunch is almost too popular and service is occasionally erratic. Nevertheless, it's one of the best bargains in town.

KNICKERS

ADDRESS: 928 Second Ave. (at 49th St.) ; 688–9488
BAR HOURS: 12 Noon–4 A.M.
FOOD: American and European specials (moderate)
CREDIT CARDS: AE BA DC MC
DRESS: Casual
SPECIAL FEATURES: Sun. brunch noon–5 P.M.
LIVELIEST TIMES: 9 P.M.–2 A.M. Tues. and Fri.

Ever since Michael Halberian took over this old Texas Guinan * speakeasy on Second Avenue and gave it the somewhat unusual name of Knickers, he's been graced with the giggles and guffaws of his regular European clientele. *Knickers* in its original Anglo-Saxon meaning refers to a particularly private feminine garment. But Mike, in an effort to reestablish nostalgia, thought he'd name the place after the short trousers or "plus fours" of the thirties.

While Mike is justly proud of his food (served in the attractive rear dining room), this is still very much a real bar. The young clientele is encouraged to sip and chat until the early hours; backgammon boards are even available when conversations become sluggish. If your "mate" is a nondrinker, Mr. Hal-

* Famous for her standard customer-greeting, "Hello, Sucker," Texas (alias Mary L. Cecilia) Guinan burst into the New York bar and nightclub scene during prohibition. She remained the rowdy, raucous, and rich queen of the city's nightlife until the more powerful forces of the underworld edged her into ignominy during the mid thirties.

berian may convert him/her with one of his Knickers "Bananas" —one of the meanest cappucinos this side of Naples.

During the day, the bar clientele is mostly drawn from the nearby advertising and publishing districts, but in the evenings after 10 P.M. the Broadway theatrical crowd often gives the place a new burst of life, which can last until closing time.

MICHAEL'S PUB

ADDRESS: 919 Third Ave. (at 55th St.); PL 8–2272
BAR HOURS: Noon–1 A.M. Mon.–Fri., 5 P.M.–1 A.M. Sat.; closed Sun.
FOOD: American (moderate)
CREDIT CARDS: AE DC
DRESS: Semiformal
SPECIAL FEATURES: Dixieland jazz every Mon. (usually with Woody Allen on clarinet), traditional and modern jazz Tues.– Sat. 9 P.M.–1 P.M., piano and singers in the Bird Cage 9:30 P.M. and 11 P.M. ($5 minimum)
LIVELIEST TIMES: 8 P.M.–midnight most evenings

Gilbert Wiest, founder and designer of the new Michael's Pub (the old one was a Michael Pearman creation on 48th St.), is to be congratulated for re-creating the atmosphere of an authentic London tavern in the heart of the midtown area. There it sits behind P. J. CLARKE's with its modest little frontage, at the base of one of many towers in this steel and concrete district—inconspicuous except for Gilbert's recent addition of a glass cube labelled appropriately, the Bird Cage. Actually the aptness of such a title can only be appreciated from the inside. Stroll through the dark doors and sit on one of the tapestry-covered chairs in this bright little room full of hanging plants and flowers. Notice the superb bronze and copper coffee machine standing in ornate glory in front of the rear wall designed to look like the outside of a medieval tavern. It's a perfect spot to enjoy the evening cabarets (pianist and singer, 9:30 P.M. and 11 P.M.) for a modest $5 minimum.

One of the main attractions here is the dixieland jazz band that plays most Monday evenings in the main dining room and features Woody Allen on clarinet. One word of warning though, this is a very different Woody Allen from the star of *Sleeper* and *Bananas* and a score of other comedies. A middle-aged matron recently asked Paul Cappa, the manager, "When's he gonna be funny then?" The point is, he's not meant to be funny here. He comes to play jazz.

165

During the remainder of the week, other jazz artists are featured in the dining room between 9 P.M. and 1 A.M., including recent appearances by Zoot Simms and George Wenn and the Newport Allstars. Michael's Pub attracts a wide range of customers. The jazz on Mondays often brings in the younger crowd, but generally there's an interesting mix of midtown executives, singles, theatricals, and a smattering of the Beautiful People who seem to have a great affection for this delightful tavern.

PEARTREES

ADDRESS: 1 Mitchell Pl. (First Ave. and 49th St.); 832–8558
BAR HOURS: Noon–4 A.M.
FOOD: American/Continental (moderate)
CREDIT CARDS: AE CB DC
DRESS: Mixed
SPECIAL FEATURES: Sun. daiquiri cocktails
LIVELIEST TIMES: Most evenings early and late

If you're not part of the in-singles crowd or a member of a UN delegation, perhaps the last time you heard about Peartrees was a few years ago when Buzzie O'Keefe, owner of the bar-restaurant, banned all midiskirts from his secluded First Avenue establishment. The furor, outrage, amusement, and mirth created by the incident became national news and put Peartrees firmly in the upper echelon of New York's "places to be seen."

Fortunately, Peartrees has a little more going for it than its reputation for unusual discrimination. It's a very inviting place with a bar overlooking the street and a delightfully secluded raised dining area. A sophisticated singles crowd (for this is by no means a "standard" singles establishment) mixes easily with Wall Street tycoons, UN personnel, and the cream of New York society.

What brings such a select group here at first seems to be a mystery. It's only a small place located at the bottom of the Beekman Tower and the decor, while pleasantly restrained, is hardly

memorable. Yet most nights of the week and particularly on Friday, it's packed with the Beautiful People, including some of the most attractive actress and model waitresses in the city. Maybe it's just as Buzzie (also owner of RUMMS), and his associate John McFadden explain: The place has that warm ambiance unique to gatherings of bright, sophisticated people.

If you'd rather avoid the weekday crush, visit Peartrees on a Sunday when the special house-cocktails are served—fresh strawberry and fresh banana daiquiris. A final note: Mr. O'Keefe has just opened a fascinating new establishment on the Brooklyn side of the East River—in a barge! It's too early to give it a review but knowing how Buzzie and success are almost synonymous terms in the Manhattan bar business, we have no doubts about its future popularity.

P. J. CLARKE'S

ADDRESS: 915 Third Ave (at 55th St.); PL 9–1650
BAR HOURS: Noon–4 A.M.
FOOD: American (inexpensive)
CREDIT CARDS: None
DRESS: Mixed
SPECIAL FEATURES: People-watching
LIVELIEST TIMES: Most evenings early and late

Clarke's has roots, and any New Yorker who hasn't been there just isn't keeping up with the Manhattan bar scene.

Built in the 1890s as a neighborhood Irish pub, it is still pretty much that, although the clientele is noticeably un-Irish. They are still from the neighborhood (which seems to encompass a great deal more territory now than it did then), and it is definitely still a pub, as well as a renowned landmark.

But in the past twenty or so years, Clarke's has become something more. It has become a bastion of informality, with good, inexpensive drink and food. And the food has always been better than you would expect to find in a typical Irish pub. That's the clue to its popularity, according to Danny Lavezzo, son of Clarke's owner. It may have a reputation as a place where the beautiful people go and where singles meet, but Mr. Lavezzo claims the reasonably priced quality food is what really keeps bringing them back.

Clarke's original tide of popularity began in an era of formality —and people came here to escape it. It was, and is, a place where behavior is the only guideline.

Fortunately its fame as a very in place and movie production locale (*Lost Weekend*) hasn't spoiled Clarke's. It's still very, very pubby. The original bar and its accoutrements, the blackboard menu, the assembled memorabilia on the walls, the cracked floor, the stained-glass transoms, and the musty fixtures, all add charm and warmth. There is another bar in the back dining room (added in 1956 by Danny's father), but reservations for the back room are mandatory—and there's a $3.00 per person minimum there. While the back is certainly more private and less raucous, the invariably packed front bar area is the most fun . . . for people meeting, people watching, good old-fashioned beer guzzling, and if you're lucky, a few stories from Frank Conefrey, one of Manhattan's best-known bartenders.

THE REIDY'S

ADDRESS: 22 E. 54th St. (between Fifth and Madison aves.);
 PL 3–2419
BAR HOURS: 10 A.M.–2 A.M.; closed Sunday
FOOD: Traditional American (inexpensive)
CREDIT CARDS: None
DRESS: Smart casual
SPECIAL FEATURES: Tradition and atmosphere
LIVELIEST TIMES: 6 P.M.–9 P.M. most evenings

We're cheating a little with this one. While the Reidy's does indeed have a bar, it's near the back beyond the front dining area and it's unusually small. However the following is so loyal and friendly and the place itself is such a venerable midtown institution, that to omit mention of it would be tantamount to sacrilege.

More than twenty-eight years ago, Maurice Reidy opened the doors of this small and very narrow establishment to a local clientele of businessmen. He offered inexpensive, traditionally prepared Irish and American cuisine, a convivial atmosphere without frills, generous drinks at the bar, and a polite staff who would grace the most exclusive of private clubs.

During subsequent years the area has been transformed out of all recognition. Few residences remain, mammoth steel and glass towers cast deep shadows in the streets, parking garages are crammed into every vacant lot, and the neighborhood hums with the fevered creativity of advertising agencies, photographic studios, publishing houses, and television studios.

At the Reidy's however, little has changed. Bill Reidy, who joined his father here in 1963, opened a second-floor dining area in 1967 and reluctantly authorized a modest price increase for the restaurant's famed entrées—corned beef and cabbage, Irish stew, broiled ham, and boiled beef. But believe it or not, you can still get a fine three-course dinner for less than $5.

The staff particularly is indicative of the Reidy's slow pace of change. Most have been around for the last twenty years and the menu even lists the names of the bartenders, each of whom seems to have his own following of loyal patrons.

To best enjoy and understand the character of this remarkable establishment you should come prepared to drink—and eat. You'll enjoy both from the moment Bill Reidy greets you at the door to the last mouthful of toast and custard pudding—the most popular dessert here.

RUMM'S TAVERN

ADDRESS: 208 E. 50th St. (near Third Ave.); 355–2424
BAR HOURS: 11 A.M.–3 A.M. Mon.–Fri.; closed Sat. and Sun.
FOOD: American (moderate)
CREDIT CARDS: AE CB DC
DRESS: Smart
LIVELIEST TIMES: Every night

Since Rumm's is directly across from Random House it seems only appropriate that we shouldn't judge this book by its cover—or rather, this bar by its façade.

For Rumm's is the least likely looking singles bar in town. Everything around it has been torn down, including the three upper stories of the building it occupies. It remains—looking somewhat like a war orphan—with slightly tattered awning, un-

painted pine door, and no neon lights, sitting smugly and enjoying its incredible reputation.

Its reputation, by the way, has seemingly spread across the country. It's become a national meeting place for the young and beautiful. The tavern doesn't advertise, yet crowds line up outside on weeknights just to get in for a drink and to rub elbows with others fighting for oxygen inside the small establishment. And it isn't even open on Saturday and Sunday.

Other than the vast crowd, what attracts people to Rumm's is that it's not a high pressure place. There are two staff men on the floor at all times to keep out the rowdies. In fact one famous Hollywood male sex symbol was unrecognized and asked to leave because he wasn't dressed appropriately. But although there is a sign stating that men must wear jackets and ties after 5 P.M., Rumm's management is flexible on this rule—to a point. But please don't test them by wearing your sweatsuit.

People also come here because they know they're not going to be ripped off. Call drinks are what you ask for—if you can get to the bar. And for those brave souls who can find their way to

172

the small back dining room, the food is good and also reasonably priced. Mostly, however, it's a Scotch drinkers paradise—especially if the Scotch drinkers are single and interested in meeting other single Scotch drinkers.

THE THREE FARTHINGS

ADDRESS: 111 E. 40th St. (between Park and Lexington aves.);
685–7631
BAR HOURS: 11:30 A.M.–2 A.M.; closed Sat. and Sun.
FOOD: Mainly American (moderate)
CREDIT CARDS: AE CB DC MC
DRESS: Informal
LIVELIEST TIMES: 6 P.M.–11 P.M. Wed.–Fri.

For those readers familiar with the London pub scene, particularly the older places around Fleet Street and the Inns of Court, the Three Farthings will appear delightfully deja vu. Even though it's located in the heart of midtown, it lacks the brazen brassiness of many of the commercialized establishments in the area. The decor is pubby, but has that element of British conservatism that makes it a distinctly pleasant haven for business people in the area. As British owner Pat Daly emphasizes, it's the people, particularly the regulars, that give the place its unique character. In fact some of the patrons are so regular that Pat has a group painting of them near the door and, on one of our visits, all but two of them were present, huddled by the bar under the stern glance of Queen Elizabeth II's portrait.

Prior to the establishment of the Three Farthings about nine years ago, this was Ricky's Restaurant, famous for steak and Italian cuisine and immortalized briefly in Brendan Behan's book on New York. Unfortunately many of the good stories about the place left with Eddie Cadena—a waiter here for twenty-five years, who recently retired. In addition to such regal accoutrements as the coronation declaration of King George V and Queen Mary, Pat displays on the walls a fine collection of old prints picked up

173

in London junk shops on his occasional visit back home. His war-time experience as a Royal Air Force radio operator is also reflected in paintings of old planes around the bar.

The Three Farthings is a tiny place, sometimes busy, sometimes very quiet. We hesitate to suggest it for a wild night on the town. Instead, come here when you're in the mood for some good food and conversation.

UNCLE CHARLIE'S SOUTH

ADDRESS: 581 Third Ave. (at 38th St.); 684–6400
BAR HOURS: 4 P.M.–4 A.M.
FOOD: None
CREDIT CARDS: None
DRESS: Casual
SPECIAL FEATURES: Low-priced drinks and hors d'oeuvres 4
    P.M.–8 P.M. nightly, hot "international" buffet, 5:30 P.M.–
    7:30 P.M. Sun.
LIVELIEST TIMES: After 10 P.M. most evenings

Robert Sloate, owner of the "friendliest gay bar in the city" explains his philosophy: "I wanted to create the kind of place where gays could meet in a club-like atmosphere without the kind of staring and hassle you find in so many other so-called gay bars."

He's succeeded. Uncle Charlie's South (no longer related to U. C. North) has a truly relaxed atmosphere. While it may not be the kind of place that "straights" would visit regularly, they're extremely welcome, and there's none of the uncomfortable tension so apparent in other more pronounced gay enclaves.

The decor is simple and pleasant, although lighting tends to be a little on the dark side. One unusual feature—there's no food other than the hot hors d'oeuvres served during the 4 P.M.–8 P.M. cocktail hour.

However, Mr. Sloate has recently opened Uncle Charlie's Restaurant a little farther down the street at 542 Third Avenue (at 36th Street) in what used to be the Old Seidelburg tavern. The heavy Germanic decor has been replaced with a delicate, yet masculine, color scheme of beige and brown with carefully placed mirrors, urns of fresh plants, and finely laid tables.

The crowd is primarily gay in the evening although it's a very gentle scene and others do not feel in the least out of place. Also, while the restaurant side is popular (there are some excellent dishes including the seafood combination, ale batter shrimp, chicken cardinalle, and veal parmigiana) the bar has a popularity

175

of its own and guests may sit and drink at the resturant tables with no obligation to eat.

Uncle Charlie's Restaurant really moves after 9 P.M. during the later weekdays. Alternatively, if you prefer a quieter atmosphere come during the cocktail hour (particularly 6 P.M.–8 P.M.) on Mondays through Wednesdays. Also note the music. It's not the standard Muzak nonsense. Instead there's a mixture of classical, contemporary, and opera.

and for
your further enjoyment...

BILL'S GAY 90's

57 E. 54th St. (between Madison and Park aves.); EL 5–0243

There's usually a minimum here ($4 weekdays, $6 Friday and Saturday), but if you're in the neighborhood and feel like watching some good old music hall acts in this tiny establishment "where nostalgia was born," give it a try. The atmosphere depends to a large extent on the customers, because the key here is participation. If you don't know or like the corny chorus songs of the twenties, then you'll feel a little out of place, especially when the nightly lantern slide quiz of old stars and entertainers gets under way, with prizes to the "super-nostalgists." If you really want to make a night of it, there's a multi-course all-inclusive dinner (that eliminates the minimum) for around $8–$11.

BILLY'S

948 First Ave. (at 53rd St.); 355–8920

We first met Billy early in the morning—a time not noted for eloquent conversation. Nevertheless, in the next hour, Mr. Condron had not only depicted the past fifty years of history in the Turtle Bay area, but had also described the prohibition days in detail, pointed out every notable feature of his small bar-restaurant (we particularly remember the original gas lamps and a superb beer pump with brass, copper, and bone handles), given us lengthy accounts of his parents, and ended up with definitive statements on gays, inflation, crime, and how to deal with difficult customers.

On subsequent occasions, however, we were able to sit quietly at the bar and enjoy the warm atmosphere of Billy's well-known

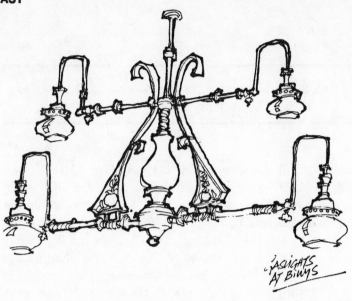

establishment. Recently the bar has become somewhat secondary to the dining area—which offers a selection of meat and seafood dishes—but it still remains a truly delightful haven of old New York.

BREW'S

156 E. 34th St. (between Third and Lexington aves.); 889–3369

Originally located between Park and Madison aves., Brew's used to be an old Irish shot 'n' beer shack. There's a photograph behind the beer pumps that gives an idea of the bar's state before it was taken over by the Brew family in the forties. The current Brew's is a far cry from the original place. At lunchtime there's a distinct cosmopolitan air as executives from the advertising and garment districts jostle elbows with the pinstripes from Wall Street over plates of scallops in wine and stuffed filet of sole with crabmeat.

Evenings, later in the week, are the best bar times. Although the place has a familiar decor (Tiffany-type lamps, red-check tablecloths, etc.) it comes alive with dixieland jazz featuring such names as Sam Margolis, Vic Dickenson, and Joe Thomas.

CHARLIE BROWN'S

45th St. (in the Pan Am Building above Grand Central Station);
   661–2520

Named after a British pub (and not the comic strip character) Charlie Brown's has pandered to the true Anglophile for more than a decade. There are English ales by the yard, half-yard, and tankard, and convincing entrées such as the steak and kidney pie, fish and chips, and roast beef with Yorkshire pudding. In the evenings, between 5 P.M. and 8 P.M. it's often packed with an interesting mix of singles and suited businessmen and offers welcome respite from the frantic scurrying in the Grand Central concourse below.

An attractive alternative to Charlie Brown's, located nearby, is the famous, and recently refurbished, Oyster Bar with its renowned selection of splendid seafood dishes. It's almost too legendary to mention—but success has not yet spoiled its reputation.

COONEY'S

152 E. 46th St. (between Third and Lexington aves.); 661–2580

November 18, 1974, saw the opening of a bubbling romp of a place in a basement along a quiet section of 46th Street. In common with other pubs in the area, it caters to a mixed and lively crowd of businessmen, professionals from nearby offices, and later in the evening, young locals.

The cocktail hour hors d'oeuvres are good, the drinks generous, the atmosphere crushed and friendly, and the food up to the normally high standards of other places owned by the two Cooney brothers (BILLYMUNK, O'CASEY'S, and MUNK'S PARK).

Journalists in the area will remember this place as Mario's Front Page. Fortunately for Cooney's the journalists (or what's left of them) still come, including many of the nearby *Playboy* magazine crowd. It's only a shame the pub is closed on weekends—the neighborhood needs a few more like this.

DAVID COPPERFIELD

322 Lexington Ave. (between 38th and 39 sts.); 686–8070

Here's another delightful British-styled pub, well known in the area for its hearty food (at lunchtime the place is invariably packed) and generous drinks. Evenings, particularly toward the end of the week, are often equally frantic but attract an interesting mix of singles, neighborhood residents, darts players—and Britishers. It's refreshing to find a place with so much nightlife on this stretch of Lexington Avenue.

GYPSY'S

1065 First Ave. (at 58th St.) 751–7520

At the time of writing, Gypsy's was a relative newcomer to the New York gay scene but had already developed a reputation as the Asti's of the liberated male. All the barmen sing and the owner, Gypsy (yes, that's his full name and yes, he claims he has gypsy origins), produces cabaret shows during the week on the small stage in the center of this unusual black- and silver-tassled bar. A recent issue of a well-known gay magazine described Gypsy's as a "totsy nite spot" and awarded a high "Four Gayolas" for its character and ambiance. Its clientele, of course, is almost exclusively gay, and if that's your thing, then you'd have a hard time finding a more bizarre yet attractive place in this part of town.

THE IRISH PAVILION

130 E. 57th St. (between Lexington and Park aves.); 759–9041

Don't be misled by the window display of hats, scarves, sweaters, and other Irish products. Behind the storefront is a delightful bar-restaurant that features fine live Irish music most evenings and, for the connoisseur, one of the best selections of Irish whiskey in Manhattan. The whole place is a transplant from Robert Moses' New York World's Fair (hence the name) and is one of the friendliest establishments in this part of town.

MAUDE'S

At the Summit Hotel (51st St. and Lexington Ave.); 735–1515

This is one of those crazy Victorian revival places à la San Francisco with all the trimmings of a west coast saloon, including young waitresses liberally displaying their matching assets. The crowd is mainly young plus others drawn from the Summit Hotel of which Maude's is a part. Cocktail hour is unusually frantic here but the hot hors d'oeuvres are good.

There are a few other instant-revival establishments in the neighborhood, including Paul Revere's and Downing Square (a little farther south along Lexington Ave.), but this is one of the more interesting—although a friend of ours had a hard time believing the price of the bottled beer.

MONK'S COURT

244 E. 51st St.   (at Second Ave.); 935–9208

If you're in the area around cocktail hour (Monday–Friday 5 P.M.–6:30 P.M.) pop into this unusual little basement restaurant designed to resemble a medieval monastic crypt. Not only are the drinks inexpensive and the atmosphere unique, but when you see those great wheels of cheese on the table near the door you'll find it hard to resist staying on for dinner. There's nothing like the smell of a ripe Stilton to set taste buds jingling.

O'CASEY'S

108 E. 41st St. (between Lexington and Park aves.); 685–6807

Particularly popular with the lunch crowd, O'Casey's is one of four places owned by Moss and Pat Cooney (BILLYMUNK, COONEY'S, and MUNK'S PARK). Decor is theatrical with a strong bias towards Irish playwrights and authors. For example, the spacious back dining room is named after Eugene O'Neill (notice his somber portrait at the doorway); downstairs is a second, more intimate, dining room with fine high-backed, green velvet chairs—the F. Scott Fitzgerald room; and finally there's the delightfully warm Sean O'Casey bar with its "James Joyce alcove"

182

and "Brendan Behan's way." Sounds a bit gimmicky, but it's not at all. In fact, compared with many of midtown's plastic palaces, it's rather restrained, yet full of atmosphere—an excellent place for lunch or an afterwork cocktail.

O'LUNNEYS

915 Second Ave. (between 48th and 49th sts.); 751–5470

If you're looking for a wild night on the town and a $3 table minimum doesn't sound excessive, come to O'Lunneys later in the week after 9 P.M. and you'll enjoy some raucous fun in the large basement bar. There's live country and western music and, for a change, dancing is not only encouraged but, at times, downright obligatory!

The upstairs area also provides live entertainment—often featuring big names in the folk singing field. There's an admission charge, but it's usually minimal and the shows can be outstanding.

PEN AND PENCIL

205 E. 45th St. (off Third Ave.); MU 2–8660

Although the bar in the Pen and Pencil is somewhat small, the place has such an intimate, clublike appeal that we couldn't bring ourselves to leave it out.

If you're into horse racing, or indeed, if you happen to own a stable (as many of the regulars here seem to do), then you'll find an instant friend in Frank, the head barman, whose knowledge of the equestrian world is matched only by his prowess as

183

a cocktail-maker. On the other hand, if baseball is more your line, talk to Kelly, one of the other barmen. Of course it could be that auto racing is really your thing. If so, ask for the owner, John Bruno (he's usually upstairs poring over fat ledgers) and don't be put off by his "I wasn't too good" line. He's raced with the best in the field, both in Britain and the United States.

The Pen and Pencil was founded in 1937 by John C. Bruno, the current owner's father. At that time it was one of the first establishments on the now-famous "steak row" and rapidly became the in place with writers and columnists from the nearby newspaper offices, including the redoubtable Walter Winchell. However, it seems that the spirit of the great newspaper era is gone. John Bruno thinks the TV reporters and anchormen of today lack the old charisma and that news programs smack of glossy superficiality. However, there's nothing superficial about his bar-restaurant. Only the best liquors are used, and the steak, aged for four weeks, is as renowned now as it was when the place opened almost forty years ago.

SCOOP

210 E. 43rd St. (between Second and Third aves.);
 MU 2–0483

While the owners, Guido Tedaldi and Gino Brugnoli, are known particularly for the quality of their Italian/American cuisine (lunchtime reservations are essential), their small, intimate bar area also attracts a regular, cosmopolitan clientele drawn from the nearby theatrical, newspaper, and advertising districts.

The walls around the restaurant are a veritable art gallery. Many of the paintings feature Italian scenes and they're all for sale. In the raised bar area, small tables are grouped on a stone floor, and over in the corner an old ticker tape machine occasionally flickers and flurries into action.

Although Scoop is often crowded, there's a relaxed ambience about the place and it's very hard not to stay for dinner, especially when Guido and Gino offer free parking, and a free bottle of anisette at the table.

THREE LIONS PUB (Tudor Hotel)

304 E. 42nd St. (between First and Second aves.); 867–3220

The strange Tudor City apartment complex with its turrets, half-timbered façade, elaborate doorways, and quiet secluded parks was built at a time when most of the surrounding development consisted of slum tenements and the United Nations site was a mess of slaughterhouses, old piers, and glue factories. It's interesting to note that the façade facing the East River is virtually windowless—in fact the whole introverted complex turned its back on the dubious neighborhood and even developed its own system of service roads and pedestrian walkways so that its high-income tenants need never be aware of the waterfront hurly-burly.

The Tudor Hotel forms part of this unusual development, and inside is this small L-shaped bar with piano and a very limited seating capacity. We mention it briefly because, being so close to the UN, it attracts an unusual cross section of diplomats, tourists, protestors, and representatives from the strangest lobby groups. On one of our visits, Oscar Running Bear and his Sioux Nation delegation had taken over the place and were attempting to persuade the somewhat alarmed pianist to provide accompaniment for the Rain Dance (a marathon spectacle that can last as long as two days!). On another occasion members of the Korean National Protestant Church were vigorously involved in making instant converts and trying to persuade a group of martini-drinkers to accompany them for cookies, cake, and coffee (and ordination, of course) at their nearby headquarters.

At least, it's different!

UPTOWN WEST

The varied texture and character of the upper west side reflects a checkered history. At far back as 1833, when the great Dakota Apartments were built overlooking the embryonic Central Park, the area was regarded as a most fashionable residential enclave. Its popularity increased with the extension of the Ninth Avenue El. Luxurious apartments and hotels developed around the major stations between 72nd Street and 104th Street, most notable of which was the baroque-styled Ansonia Hotel at 73rd Street and Broadway. The laying out of Frederick Law Olmsted's great designs for Central Park and Riverside Park during the 1860s and 70s only served to increase the area's attraction, and the construction of the north campus of Columbia University in the 1890s seemed to set the seal of quality and permanency.

Unfortunately, the wealthy residents of the upper west side overlooked the fact that Manhattan was still in the process of growing northwards. Many believed they were safely ensconsed from the tidal waves of immigrants that had engulfed so many of the city's once-fashionable neighborhoods, transforming within a few short months, quiet dignified streets into tumultuous slums. They should have seen the signs. As early as 1860 speculative developers were filling empty lots around Lincoln Square with cheap tenements for mainly Irish immigrants. As the El moved northwards, so did the slums. Nothing could stem their tide. Within a short period, the Irish were joined, in a now-familiar pattern, by Germans, Jews, and Ukrainians. By the early twentieth century, most of the district was badly blighted, and with the onset of the depression the last ramparts of the rich gave way. In came the Puerto Ricans, the Haitians, the Dominicans, and the Orientals—all creating vibrant mini-neighborhoods complete with their own stores, churches, and cultures. Within a short period of less than sixty years, the area was transformed beyond recognition.

There was, however, great pride and concern for the area by its residents. This was the primary factor leading to the upper west side's renaissance following World War II. Massive investment in public housing (including one notable failure by Manhattan Town, Inc.), coupled with an uncanny ability on the part of the local population to form action-oriented block groups, prevented further major deterioration. The ambitious Lincoln Center project begun in 1962 removed some of the worst remaining tenements and brought new cultural life to the lower part of the west side, which in turn attracted a rapid influx of West Village and East Village residents.

Today the area is one of the most vibrant, cosmopolitan, and culturally dynamic neighborhoods in Manhattan. Old, time-worn stores have been converted into a dazzling array of boutiques, underground book shops, antique outlets, and coffee houses. Murky Irish saloons have been gutted and refurbished to cater to the young artists, writers, and intellectuals who fill the renovated brownstones and nineteenth-century apartment structures between Lincoln Center and Columbia University. From what was once an elite enclave of the rich has emerged a new "Village," or rather, a series of "Villages" for the youth of Manhattan.

Bar connoisseurs will quickly recognize that the upper west side is divided into four relatively distinct zones. Perhaps most interesting, because of its recent emergence as an upper-east-side-styled neighborhood, is lower Columbus Avenue near Lincoln Center. Although it contains a few traditional taverns that have managed to withstand the cultural onslaught of the Center and nearby ABC studios (McGlade's and Cafe des Artistes are fine examples), many pubs in the area cater to a unique combination of young neighborhood residents (often loosely categorized as "singles"), theatricals, celebrities, and regular evening waves of avid culture buffs. Dazzels, Chipps, Ghenghiz Khan's Bicycle, and the three O'Neal establishments (O'Neal's Baloon, O'Neal Bros., and the Ginger Man) are all fine examples of new or refurbished taverns that have, within a few short years, developed a unique sense of permanency.

Further up Broadway, in the heart of the new Village around 72nd Street, is another collection of recently converted establishments including the Allstate Cafe, Mrs. J's Sacred Cow, and the

Copper Hatch. The latter was once a popular coffee house and still retains much of its old flavor, particularly in the sidewalk porch café. Contrary to popular opinion, by the way, the recent flurry of porch café construction, particularly in Greenwich Village and the upper east side, is by no means a new concept. Old lithographs of Manhattan indicate that as far back as 1850 such sidewalk extensions formed an integral part of the Bowery's gardens and beer halls.

The third major tavern zone on the upper west side caters primarily to Columbia University students, although recently, such places as the Abbey Pub, the Balcony, the Gold Rail, Hanratty's, the Library, and Teacher's have begun to attract regular evening patronage by residents of Greenwich Village. Without exception these are lively taverns and the coffee house flavor of Hanratty's and the Balcony seems particularly appropriate to the area.

Finally, there are the jazz taverns around Columbus Avenue and 90th Street—Mikell's, Strykers, and the Cellar, that provide some of the best music by renowned performers in the city. The clientele is truly cosmopolitan, although most remarkable of all in terms of patronage and entertainment, is the Music Room (Broadway and 112th Street), featuring live classical music and opera. This small pub is the most significant indication of the upper west side's successful renaissance.

THE ABBEY PUB

ADDRESS: 237 W. 105th St. (at Broadway); 850–1630
BAR HOURS: 4 P.M.–2 A.M. Sun.–Thurs., 4 P.M.–4 A.M. Fri. and
   Sat.
FOOD: American (moderate)
CREDIT CARDS: None
DRESS: Casual
SPECIAL FEATURES: Cocktail hour 4 P.M.–7 P.M.—drinks $1
   and beers 50¢, monthly parties
LIVELIEST TIMES: 8:30 P.M.–2 A.M. Wed.–Sat.

The Abbey, with its subdued, well-manicured air and inviting atmosphere, was one of the first watering holes along this particular stretch of Broadway. Owners Michael Kearney and Paul Munsinger, who used to be vice-president of a brokerage house on Wall Street, decided three years ago that it was time the publess, yet populous, neighborhood had a suitable social gathering place of its own. They were right. The Abbey was a roaring success even before it opened (locals started to frequent the place long before the tables and chairs arrived) and subsequently sparked off a spate of bar building in the area.

Inside, it's restrained but delightful. A varied crowd—all ages and races—relaxes in surroundings of dark wood panelling, stained glass (from Munsinger's collection), and a proliferation of green plants nurtured by spotlights (very necessary in this basement location). It's recently become a popular hangout for Columbia students wanting to escape the college scene for a few hours, before-and-after the theatre crowd attending productions at the Equity Library Theatre on 103rd Street, and also a healthy contingent of Village residents looking for a different kind of bar scene.

The most regular customer, however, is the Abbey Pub ghost who apparently stops by in the early afternoon before the pub opens to toast himself, and perhaps his equally invisible companions, with the bar-brand Scotch. Both Munsinger and Kearney have heard its footsteps and swear that there's always less in the bottle after the eerie sounds have gone. They hypothesize that the visitor may be Leary, a well-known local Irishman who lived in the building for many years. And unless he changes his taste to Chivas Regal, they consider him a welcome, if somewhat unusual, feature of the place.

THE CAFÉ DES ARTISTES

===

ADDRESS: 1 W. 67th St. (near Central Park West); TR 7-3343
BAR HOURS: Noon–1 A.M. Mon.–Fri., 5 P.M.–1 A.M. Sat., closed
   Sun.
FOOD: Varied (moderate)
CREDIT CARDS: AE CB DC
DRESS: Smart casual
SPECIAL FEATURES: Murals by Howard Chandler Christy
LIVELIEST TIMES: Mainly around cocktail hour most days

===

Entering the Café Des Artistes is like walking into an old, slightly faded, yet warm-toned sepia print. Not only do the gold tablecloths add to this effect, but they bring out the softly glowing colors of the magnificent murals covering almost every inch of the wall at this most unusual café. Painted by Howard Chandler Christy in 1934 (upper level) and 1942 (lower level), they depict beautiful cavorting female nudes (and one lone male) executed in the romantic pre-Raphaelite style of that era. By today's standards the subject matter with its gentle erotic overtones is both tasteful and pleasing—however, those were certainly not the adjectives used by many critics in those less enlightened days.

The Café is on the bottom floor of what was the Hotel Des Artistes, and is now the Des Artistes Co-op. Christy, who was also famed as a portrait and landscape painter, resided in the hotel for thirty-five years, and in fact was its first tenant on April 1, 1917.

Today the Café Des Artistes looks much as it did during the forties. The first restaurant in the Lincoln Center area, it has only been slightly refurbished with occasional fresh coats of ceiling paint and other minor clean-up projects. The murals have been restored four times.

Surrounded by television studios, many of its patrons are involved in the media, and it's not unusual for Harry Reasoner or Howard Cosell to stop by for an evening cocktail. Owner Romeo Sterlini appears to know everyone that comes in and has a remarkable memory for names and the jobs, idiosyncrasies, and individual tastes associated with those names. Of course, he's had plenty of time to learn. His father was bartender here, prior to purchasing the Café in 1934. Romeo starting working here in 1941, and he became a partner with co-owner Charles Turner in 1949. They both remember the Café long before the ABC studios and Lincoln Center existed and are particularly proud of those few remaining regulars who have been coming by for thirty-five years.

The Café Des Artistes is an ageless and beautiful establishment —one of the gems of Manhattan.

THE CELLAR RESTAURANT

ADDRESS: 70 W. 95th St. (at Columbus Ave.); 866–1200
BAR HOURS: 4 P.M.–2 A.M. Sun.–Thurs., 4 P.M.–4 A.M. Fri. and Sat.
FOOD: Soul, American, European (moderate)
CREDIT CARDS: AE MC DC
DRESS: Semiformal
SPECIAL FEATURES: Live jazz and soul music
LIVELIEST TIMES: 9 P.M.–3 A.M. Wed.–Sat.

The Cellar is different things to different people. It's a place where both blacks and whites meet and drink, where live music is heard, where businessmen relax after work, where singles dally expectantly, and where neighbors get together.

Situated at the bottom of one of those great, grey apartment complexes that poke at the sky, the Cellar is also the pride of its owner, Howard Johnson. He makes a special effort to get to know his customers and to make them feel welcome and comfortable. He also makes an effort to ensure that they are entertained by some of the best and most famous names in jazz, including Ron Carter and Earl May.

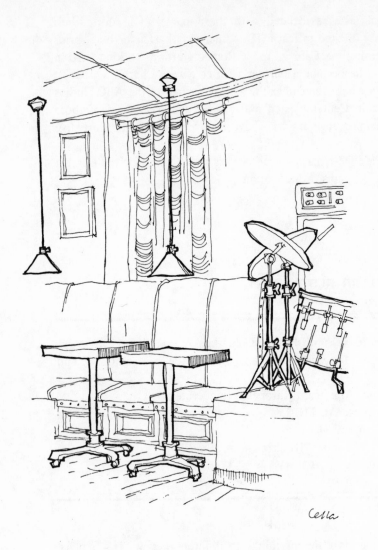

Cella

When the music is going, from 10 P.M. to 4 A.M. Wednesday through Saturday, a cabaret atmosphere prevails. Low lights hang over each table, decorations are kept minimal, and the focus is on the bandstand at the front of the room. During these hours, there's also a two-drink minimum at the tables.

If the tables don't suit you, sit at the bar and munch potato chips and peanuts. And if you want to make a night of it, stop by between 5 P.M. and 8 P.M. for free hors d'oeuvres, then enjoy a dinner of French, Italian, Chinese, or soul food before the show.

DAZZELS

ADDRESS: 180 Columbus Ave. (at 68th St.); 874–9899
BAR HOURS: 11:30 A.M.–4 A.M.
FOOD: American and European (moderate)
CREDIT CARDS: None
DRESS: Casual
SPECIAL FEATURES: Sat. and Sun. brunch
LIVELIEST TIMES: 9 P.M.–2 A.M. Wed.–Fri.

This whole area at Columbus Ave., near Lincoln Center, is beginning to take on many of the characteristics of the upper east side and Dazzels is only one of a number of pleasant places to spend a lively evening .

The scene varies considerably throughout the day. At lunchtime there's a steady influx of business types and a large contin-

gent of patrons from the ABC headquarters located at Columbus and 68th Street. Dinner time brings the Lincoln Center crowd, and it's only in the later evening that the younger neighborhood regulars begin to take over.

Until a couple of years ago Dazzels (owner Walter Borchers has no idea why he called it that) was a solid Irish tavern attracting the older neighborhood residents and with a flavor that can still be found in nearby McGlade's.

The addition of a bright porch, a young staff, exotic cocktails (beware of the Louisiana Lady), and such attractions as the Monday night Gemini dinner (two for the price of one) have attracted a very friendly crowd. The place is really comfortable and the decor is pleasant but not overly contrived. Whenever they feel in the mood, Walter and his German manager, York Kane, throw impromptu parties with free food for all. Also, when the Harkness Ballet School was having financial problems, they organized an immensely successful "event" to raise urgently needed funds.

GENGHIZ KHAN'S BICYCLE

ADDRESS: 197 Columbus Ave. (at 69th St.); 592–2138
BAR HOURS: 11:30 A.M.–3 A.M.
FOOD: Turkish/American (moderate)
CREDIT CARDS: AE MC
DRESS: Semiformal
SPECIAL FEATURES: Live entertainment, backgammon tables
LIVELIEST TIMES: 8 P.M.–1 A.M. most evenings

Gamal El Zagby, the award-winning architect who designed this unusual bar-restaurant, created the ultimate white environment: bar, tables, walls, and ceilings. That way, according to owner Kemal Sonmez, the people are the decoration. "The white interior gives the best background for human beings," Sonmez says. But even without people, the design is exciting—so exciting, that it was featured on the cover of *Interior* magazine and continues to draw admiring architects and designers. (After visiting scores of Irish-revival taverns with their sawdust and red-check

tablecloth decor, we found this place a most pleasant and welcome relief.)

Other members of the clientele here, while appreciating the appealing decor, may stop by to sample the extensive Middle Eastern cuisine, have the grounds of their Turkish coffee read, or play backgammon on the balcony above the dining and drinking area The nine tables on the balcony all have recessed backgammon boards, and there are backgammon tournaments held here every Sunday from about 2:30 P.M. For the novice, there are free backgammon lessons on Monday nights from about 6 P.M.

Wednesday through Sunday evenings there is live music, and belly dancers or other entertainers perform at 10 P.M.—all without a cover charge or minimum. Now, what does all this have to do with a bicycle? Nothing, except that Genghiz Khan's Bicycle is the name of a screenplay written by a Turkish author, and owner Sonmez is a filmmaker. In fact, the singer who regularly entertains customers at the restaurant will be starring in Mr. Sonmez's film, currently in production.

197

THE GOLD RAIL

ADDRESS: 2850 Broadway (between 110th and 111th sts.) ; MO 2-
4704
BAR HOURS: 8 A.M.–4 A.M. daily
FOOD: American (moderate)
CREDIT CARDS: None
DRESS: Very informal
SPECIAL FEATURES: Bar from New York Pavilion 1939 World's
Fair
LIVELIEST TIMES: Most evenings from dinner time onwards

If you're tired of being stuffed into crowded bars and yearn for a little nostalgia with your beer, you'll find lots of room and history in the Gold Rail. The great wooden bar with its gleaming brass footrail, the back-bar, and most of the elaborate lighting fixtures, are all from the New York Pavilion at the 1939 World's Fair. The tavern itself has seen the neighborhood through sixty years of change, reflected in the clientele composed primarily of Columbia University students. Management admits that without the students the place would not have survived, even though people from the area (including entire families) come by in droves for dinner in the evening, and businessmen from nearby banks and hospitals hold enthusiastic and regular pinball contests here. In the latter instance the barmen are so busy verifying scores that serving drinks becomes a very secondary occupation.

Many of the staff are from Columbia, with the exception of Casey, the daytime bartender, who's been here for fifteen years, and the two chefs who have put in twenty-three and twenty-five years respectively. They've seen a lot of their regular clientele grow up, including two former Columbia students who used to work here and who are now assistant district attorneys in Manhattan and the Bronx. Whenever there's a reunion at the college, the old customers invariably come back to relive their former escapades for a few hours.

The present owner, Joe Perrothers, is himself an old customer. Born in the neighborhood, he used to drink at the Gold Rail when he was a kid and now watches, maybe a little enviously, the new generation of students who give this place so much of its character and flavor.

HANRATTY'S

ADDRESS: 732 Amsterdam Ave. (at 96th St.); 864–4224
BAR HOURS: 11:30 A.M.–1 A.M. daily
FOOD: American (moderate)
CREDIT CARDS: None
DRESS: Casual
SPECIAL FEATURES: Photography exhibits, Sat. and Sun. brunch
    noon–3 P.M.
LIVELIEST TIMES: 8 P.M.–midnight Wed.–Fri.

Hanratty's seems to be a place where everyone feels at home. And everyone here means Spanish, black, and anglo neighbors— all having a remarkably good time.

It used to be an old Irish bar, but the neighborhood changed in character so everything was torn out, except the original seventy-year old bar itself, and the new Hanratty's emerged five years ago. Now it is clean and appealing and has the easy look and feel of a coffee house.

Exhibitions of work by different photographers hang on one wall and are changed regularly by Lee Romero, a free-lance photographer formerly with the *New York Times,* who decides whose works are to be shown. When there's a void, he simply puts up his own excellent photographs.

During the dinner hours drinkers may only use the bar; but at other times the tables are freely available. Once you decide where to sit the only remaining decision is what to drink in this beer-lover's paradise. Bass Ale and dark Würzbürger are only two of the six beers on tap, so you could find this decision the most difficult. We suggest, however, that if you select a beer, don't mix it with the Hanratty specialty—a Tequila Sunrise. The result could be a very personal sunset.

THE LIBRARY

ADDRESS: 2475 Broadway (at 92nd St.); 799–4860
BAR HOURS: Noon–3 P.M. and 5 P.M.–midnight Mon.–Thurs.,
noon–3 P.M. and 5 P.M.–1 A.M. Fri.-Sat., Sun. noon–4 P.M.
and 5 P.M.–midnight (Note two-hour closures)
FOOD: American and European (moderate)
CREDIT CARDS: AE MC
DRESS: Casual
SPECIAL FEATURES: Books, books, books; Sun. brunch noon–4
P.M.
LIVELIEST TIMES: 9 P.M.–closing Wed.–Sun.

Owner Stewart Steinberg doesn't know where they come from or why they even started coming to his book-lined neighborhood bar. But on Fridays, the place is jammed with singles. They flock in and flock out that one day of the week. Strangers in the night, etc. . . . Most other times, the Library may be busy with neighborhood people: actors, writers, or artists. It's a relaxing place, and except for the conspicuous lack of "Silence" signs and the abundance of ashtrays, it looks remarkably like a branch of the city library—misshelved books, lousy lighting, rickety chairs, scratched up tables.

The rows of books on the seemingly endless bookcases were not selected by Mr. Steinberg for his friends' edification, however. Most of them were purchased for a few cents a pound from the Salvation Army. The ones stacked on the back bar have been sent to him by friends in the publishing business, so they are kept out of reach. Apparently the accessibility of many of the other volumes has presented temptation too difficult for some customers to resist—hence the lack of classics within grabable range.

Imitation is supposed to be the sincerest form of flattery, and the decor of the Library has been widely imitated. But it is unlikely that any other place can or will be able to capture the casual mood and friendly atmosphere here. Anyway, Mr. Steinberg is not worried about the competition. He's doing all right and has even managed to put some time into his original calling—acting. He can be easily spotted at any audition—he's the one with an old book in his hand.

MIKELL'S

ADDRESS: 760 Columbus Ave. (at 97th St.); 864-8832
BAR HOURS: 3 P.M.–4 A.M. (1 P.M.–4 A.M. Sat. and Sun.)
FOOD: Seafood, steaks and soulfood (moderate)
CREDIT CARDS: AE BA CB DC MC
DRESS: Casual
SPECIAL FEATURES: Live jazz from 10 P.M. ($1 cover and two-drink minimum)
LIVELIEST TIMES: From 10 P.M. Thurs.–Sat.

Ever since 52nd Street died in the fifties, taking with it all those renowned jazz bars—Famous Door, Birdland, Downbeat, and a score of others, the scene has fragmented throughout Manhattan. However, in recent years there's been an influx of jazz on the upper west side. Many of the clubs only last a few months, but Mikell's has, in its four years of existence, become a landmark, attracting such noted regulars as Chico Hamilton, Joe Farrell, Junior Mance, and Roy Haynes.

It's a most unusual establishment located way up near the Park West Village complex at the corner of a modern, low-rise commercial strip. On the outside there's a rough wood porch and a torn green canopy that flaps erratically above the door. No fuss, no glitter, no flashing signs. Inside is a wide expanse of bar area and the plain stained-wood decor and small dining tables in the porch area give it a friendly, homey atmosphere.

From 7 P.M., when the dinner crowd arrives to feast on an interesting selection of seafood, steak, and soul food dishes (and an excellent chili), Mikell's becomes progressively busier. By 11 P.M. it's a congenial melting pot of students, locals, blacks, caucasians, people from the Village, and celebrities from the world of jazz and show business. The music romps on until the early hours of the morning and later in the week, when Mike Mikell usually introduces the bigger names, 4 A.M. always comes too soon.

THE MUSIC ROOM

ADDRESS: 2871 Broadway (between 111th and 112th sts.); 866–2018

BAR HOURS: 11 A.M.–2 A.M. Tues.–Sat., 11 A.M.–midnight Sun. and Mon.

FOOD: American and European (moderate)

CREDIT CARDS: BA MC

DRESS: Informal

SPECIAL FEATURES: Live classical music after 7 P.M., Sun. brunch noon–3 P.M. with folk music

LIVELIEST TIMES: 8 P.M.–11 P.M. Wed.–Fri. and Sun. brunch

At first there doesn't appear to be anything special about this renovated mini-supermarket. It's small, clean, and plain with hanging plants scattered randomly, a bar to one side of the room, and twenty or so tables on the other side and at the back. But look more closely—in the middle of the room is a full-sized concert harp! Maybe on another day the harp won't be there. But you can be assured that at 7 P.M. on any evening, some instrument on which classical music is played will be the focal point of the Music Room—maybe a lute, bassoon, clarinet, violin, or the fine eighty-year old Steinway piano—a permanent fixture of the place.

The appeal and artistry of the performers—many of them graduates of Juilliard—has attracted patrons from all over Manhattan. During the day it's mainly a local neighborhood tavern, but at night when the performances start, the crowd changes. Classical music lovers turn out, knowing they can hear fine music without paying a cover change or meeting a minimum. They are simply reminded that a basket for contributions is by the door, and on Friday and Saturday evenings when chamber groups are normally featured, that basket brims.

Even during its short two-year existence the Music Room has gained the respect and attention of many of the city's better-known reviewers, who often attend the intimate concerts looking for new and promising talent. The standard of music is remarkably high, but owner Shankar Ghosh (ex-journalist and publisher) encourages any aspiring artist to pop in for an impromptu audition.

On Sundays, along with the brunch, there's a change of pace with live folk music. The Music Room once again becomes a center for young local residents and the atmosphere is delightfully casual. Whichever kind of music you prefer, this is a fascinating place to spend a few hours dining and drinking. By the way, note the superb art deco bar. Mr. Ghosh and friends moved it piece by piece from an old Staten Island tavern and, along with the harp, it gives the Music Room a truly unique and fascinating flavor.

O'NEALS' BALOON

ADDRESS: 48 W. 63rd St. (at Columbus Ave.); 765–5577
BAR HOURS: 11:30 A.M.–1 A.M. daily
FOOD: American (inexpensive)
CREDIT CARDS: None
DRESS: Mixed
SPECIAL FEATURES: Sidewalk café
LIVELIEST TIMES: 7 P.M.–11 P.M. most evenings

If you've heard of O'Neals' Baloon across from the Lincoln Center but have never been there, you're probably in for a surprise. First, it is not a pretentious place, although it does cater to both the patrons and the performers at the Center. Second, the prices

205

are not outrageous. They are, in fact, downright reasonable, and reflect the menu's unexpected preponderance of hamburgers. Third, it's "baloon" with one *L*, not two. That's because the name originally intended for the place was O'Neals' Saloon. All the signs were made before it was discovered that there was a New York law prohibiting use of the word *saloon* in a tavern's name. So rather than redo everything, the name was changed to "baloon." Or at least, that's how the story goes.

The interior is attractive, but simple, with wooden tables and chairs and only one particularly outstanding decorative touch: a large mural painted by artist Bob Crowl, depicting the O'Neal brothers, their families, friends, members of the O'Neal organization, principals of the New York City Ballet; plus selected dancers from other companies. Space is still available for new friends and/or family to be painted in, and this is done regularly. To date, however, no one has been painted over!

Most employees at O'Neals' are aspiring artists, musicians, writers, etc., and it is standard policy here to hire those involved in the arts. But the conversation and chatter is wide-ranging, so don't feel badly if you don't know your Toscanini from your Picasso. It's not a singles spot, but definitely a place to meet interesting people.

TEACHER'S

ADDRESS: 2249 Broadway (between 80th and 81st sts.); 787–3500
BAR HOURS: 11:30 A.M.–2 A.M. daily
FOOD: American (moderate)
CREDIT CARDS: AE DC MC
DRESS: Casual
SPECIAL FEATURES: Good selection of California wine by glass or carafe, Sun. brunch noon–5 P.M.
LIVELIEST TIMES: 8 P.M.–1 A.M. Tues.–Sat.

Olga Klos, manager of Teacher's, stresses the fact that the upper west side has been constantly improving over recent years.

The pub itself is ample evidence. Not too long ago it was one of those gray neighborhood bars, characteristic of the one-time marginal nature of the area, with a seedy decor and a clientele to match.

Now, in its splendidly improved state (note the fine oil paintings on the wall that are usually for sale) it's a place where the famous go to be unrecognized and unpretentious, dressed in anything from blue jeans to tuxedos, and indeed the casual atmosphere has proved such an attraction that the place is invariably crowded, even in mid-afternoon.

For those of us not usually concerned about avoiding frantic fans, the primary appeal of Teacher's is value—reasonably priced drinks and high-quality yet simply prepared food. There's a friendly, clublike spirit about the place; women, singles or in groups, can come here without fear of undue hassle. And in the evenings it's often popular with entire families who come to gorge themselves on Teacher's gigantic hamburgers. Generally, however, the crowd is made up of young professionals who huddle around the butcher block tables seeking relaxation during or after a busy day. The success of Teacher's is based on the fact that they can find it here.

THE WEST END

ADDRESS: 2911 Broadway (between 113th and 114th sts.); 666–8750
BAR HOURS: 8 A.M.–4 A.M. Mon.–Sat., noon–4 A.M. Sun.
FOOD: American (inexpensive)
CREDIT CARDS: None
DRESS: Casual
SPECIAL FEATURES: Live jazz, the "Blue Lion Cocktail"
LIVELIEST TIMES: 10 P.M.–3 A.M. Thurs.–Sat.

The West End blends in so well with the adjoining shops and supermarket that it's hard to tell where one starts and the others end—especially when signs in the window advertising dinner

prices at the West End seem to be the work of the same artist who prepares the lettuce and instant coffee sale signs next door.

Even after you discover the entrance to the West End, your confusion may continue. Inside you're faced with a cafeteria counter to the left and an enormous four-sided bar in the middle of the room that would look more appropriate in a student's union, particularly since it's invariably surrounded by students from nearby Columbia University who eat, drink, and occasionally even hold impromptu classes here. Students have been coming to the West End, established in 1901, for years, and Jack Kerouac and Allen Ginsberg spent many of their undergraduate days here. Ginsberg still pops in for an occasional—and unannounced— poetry reading, according to Sidney Roberts, who has owned the West End for twenty-five years.

In 1974 Roberts introduced a jazz room to complement the two large dining and drinking areas. There are four sets played every night running from 9 P.M. until 1 A.M. during the week and between 10 P.M. and 2 A.M. on the weekends. If you don't want to pay the $1.50 minimum at the tables in the jazz room, you can sit in the other areas and just listen to some great music by such artists as Eddie Durham, Sam Woodyard, George Kelley, Tiny Grimes, the ever fresh Mable Godwin, and occasional appearances by Sammy Price (King of Charleston Boogie Woogie). You might even try a "Blue Lion"—named by a student during the unrest at Columbia, when it was said that even the Columbia lion was sad. The concoction created by Roberts to match that name consists of rum, lemon juice, blue Curaçao, and sugar and tastes far better than it sounds.

and for
your further enjoyment...

ALLSTATE CAFE

250 W. 72nd St. (at Broadway); 874–1883

A most successful remodeling job! This one-time hard-drinker's hangout now has an almost collegiate look with its young denim-clad customers eating hamburgers, drinking beer and wine, and listening to the jukebox. It's brighter and a little more bouncy than the nearby COPPER HATCH and attracts a number of film and stage celebrities—particularly on Sundays when there's live chamber music with brunch.

THE BALCONY

2772 Broadway (at 107th St.); 850–3050

Until the Balcony arrived on the upper west side, the neighborhood lacked a pub with that real street-front flavor, so popular in areas like Greenwich Village. Its tall windows overlook the passing scene and tiny triangular Strauss Park. Patrons sitting at the bar or small tables have a remarkable selection of beers from which to choose (the India Pale Ale is a favorite) and the atmosphere is a little more tranquil than in some of the raucous places farther up Broadway. Decor is simple—bare brick and wood (with a crazy, purposeless balcony above the bar), and the taped music, mainly jazz and classical, makes a pleasant change.

CHIPP'S PUB

150 Columbus Ave. (at 67th St.); 874–8415

Close to DAZZELS is another popular tavern in this Lincoln Center zone of Columbus Avenue. It's a narrow, intimate establishment with a small porch café and a special, slightly refined ambience. Like most other places in the neighborhood, it attracts the pre- and after-theatre crowd, but the locals come into their own after 11 P.M. There's an interesting Italian/American menu and cocktails are unusually generous.

COPPER HATCH

247 W. 72nd St. (at Broadway); 799–8377

Reflecting its past fame as a coffee house, the Copper Hatch still serves a splendid selection of authentic preparations including espresso, cappucino, Irish coffee, Mexican coffee (with Kahlua), and Jamaican coffee (with Tia Maria). It also has a café from which patrons can look out across vases of fresh flowers at the passing street scene or peer down into the attractive, slightly nautical flavored bar and restaurant area with its model sailing ships, hatch covers, and a superb copper awning. It's mostly for young couples and a quiet regular crowd, with the exception of one dear lady who insists on presenting her life history in full detail each time she visits, to tolerant, but slightly bored, listeners. The menu is limited, but the place is renowned for its fine hamburgers served on English muffins and Yugoslavian meatballs with rice.

THE GINGER MAN

51 West 64th St. (at Broadway); SC 4–7272

For another sample of the O'Neal brothers' talent (see O'NEALS' BALOON and LANDMARK) but in a more inviting neighborhood, try the Ginger Man near Lincoln Center. It was their first venture in the dining and drinking business and is regarded by many as one of the few authentic French cafés in Manhattan.

Because of its location it caters primarily to Lincoln Center patrons and the mood is most relaxed. The decor is superb (by Mesdames O'Neal we're told) and it's the kind of place that invites lengthy dawdling over a glass of wine, some Irish coffee, or the fine French provincial food prepared by chef Daniel Millien.

McGLADES

154 Columbus Ave. (at 67th St.); 874–9638

This old, tradition-bound tavern never ceases to impress us. In an area where the bars are rapidly taking on many of the more flamboyant upper east side characteristics, McGlades remains just as it has been for many years—a true neighborhood pub attracting an older clientele. There are times, of course, particularly pre and after theatre, when patronage becomes a little more diversified, but during the day and late at night, it's the same old faces and the same, slightly conservative atmosphere that makes McGlades such an interesting tavern.

MRS. J'S SACRED COW

228 W. 72nd St. (near Broadway); 873–4067

Mrs. J's Sacred Cow, just down the block from the ALLSTATE CAFE, is a little more of a restaurant than a pub, priding itself on its prime steaks and fresh fish and boasting an unusual art deco dining room on the second floor. There's a beautiful bar however, at the front, and an enclosed sidewalk café. And the whole place has that refined, established grace that comes from twenty-eight years of existence and a loyal and regular clientele, many of whom are show business celebrities. A pianist plays in the dining room every night from 8 P.M. and patrons can listen from the bar, or join in with the singing waitresses at the dining room tables where there's a $3.50 per person minimum. It's a lovely way to spend an evening.

O'NEAL BROS.

269 Columbus Ave. (at 72nd St.); 362–2700

Here's another O'Neal establishment (see O'NEALS' BALOON, the LANDMARK TAVERN, and THE GINGER MAN). The brothers really seem to have that Midas touch—all their taverns and restaurants have different and distinct characteristics and all are amazingly successful. This particular place, located on the lively lower section of Columbus near Lincoln Center, does a roaring singles business in the evening in addition to catering to theatregoers. It has a pleasant neighborhood atmosphere, complete with backgammon tables, dart boards, and darts teams that hold tournaments every Tuesday evening.

P.S. 77

355 Amsterdam Ave. (at 77th St.); 873–6930

On the corner of a heavily trafficked street, in an old run-down neighborhood, and surrounded by tiny shops, is P.S. 77. It's not an old schoolhouse, although several schools are located nearby; it's simply a scoured, scrubbed, and polished restaurant-bar that opened in April of 1974.

During its brief existence in this incongruous setting, P.S. 77 has managed to attract trade from all over the city, including regular contingents of the discriminating Lincoln Center crowd. The bar is small, but you can get a ten-ounce glass of California wine for $1 or an enormous martini, and there are plans to introduce live music. It's a place to watch for developments, but already the French and European cuisine has gained P.S. 77 a devoted following.

215

STRYKERS

103 W. 86th St. (at Columbus Ave.); 874–8754

Not far down the avenue from MIKELL'S is Strykers, another mecca of good jazz in the neighborhood. You'll have to look carefully. It's tucked away in a cramped brownstone basement and draws minimal attention to itself. The Lee Konitz Trio (see GREGORY'S) plays here and other well-known names include Chet Baker, David Samuel, and the guitar duo Chuck Wayne and Joe Puma. There's no cover or minimum, and if you like a dark basement atmosphere this is an ideal place. Music starts around 9 P.M. every night of the week, and it's best to call in advance and check on the program.

UPTOWN EAST

This thriving, vibrant district possesses more pubs and taverns in relation to its size than any other part of Manhattan. This can be explained to some extent by the once-predominant German population in the community of Yorkville, and the fact that many of New York's breweries were once located east of Third Avenue above 90th Street. However, the area never took on the wild characteristics of the Bowery, another major German/Irish enclave. Instead, its beer houses and restaurants became relatively restrained social centers for a neighborhood populace of Hungarians, Czechs, Germans, Austrians, and other representatives of eastern Europe's myriad subcultures. The streets were littered with pork shops and bakeries, and the aroma of unfamiliar dishes wafted over the narrow sidewalks—goulash, paprika-boiled meats, spätzle, strudels, schnitzels, sauerbraten, wursts, hoppel-poppel, and exotic versions of roast duck and goose.

The community of Yorkville, founded during the 1790s, began to develop significantly after the opening of the Harlem River Railroad in 1834. However, it was not until the 1880s when elevated railroad links were developed with the city further to the south, that the real influx began in earnest. By 1910 Yorkville boasted a proportionately larger German population than any other city in the world except Berlin. Some were new immigrants fresh from Europe, but most were families from the lower east side who, having clawed their way up the economic ladder, could afford to leave that rapidly deteriorating ghetto.

Of course Yorkville, centered around Third Avenue between 83rd and 89th streets, occupied only a small portion of the upper east side. To the west between Central Park and Park Avenue were the great mansions of New York's wealthy families. The

217

Astors resided in a vast chateau on the corner of 66th Street complete with elaborate mansard roofs and Versailles trimmings. A little further to the north was the Frick mansion, which today houses the magnificent private art collection of Henry Clay Frick, the Pittsburgh industrialist. Other equally extravagant residences included Edward Harkness' Roman palace, the Louis XII-styled Stuyvesant mansion, and the Lous XIII Vanderbilt mansion. Needless to say, the area possessed few public taverns. Most of the side streets were occupied by stables or servants' quarters, and the lords and ladies of Fifth Avenue made it clear that they had no desire to attract the riffraff from adjoining neighborhoods.

In complete contrast, the area east of Yorkville and Third Avenue was a continuation of the Turtle Bay–East River slum. Vast breweries and smoking factories were surrounded by overcrowded tenements occupied by the Irish, whose main contribution to the city in those days seemed to be cheap labor, and a remarkable capacity for human endurance under the worst living conditions imaginable. The café society and wealthy bohemians living on nearby Lenox Hill, could rant, write pamphlets, and deliver fiery diatribes regarding the abominable plight of these immigrants, but change came all too slowly, and countless lives were wasted away in the gin mills, grog shops, and stale-beer dives along First and Second avenues.

Today, except for the still-rigid barrier of Park Avenue that separates the residences of the elite from the remainder of the district, the upper east side possesses a remarkable homogeneity. While relatively little remains of the old Yorkville and the Irish slums, in the last decade the area has become a bedroom for young, often single students, actors, models, professionals, and teachers. While it lacks the more intense intellectual characteristics of the "New Village" on the upper west side, it has a unique, light-hearted, "damn-tomorrow" flavor that is reflected in its discotheques, restaurants, boutiques, and well-known "singles" taverns—Friday's, Dr. Generosity, Hudson Bay, the Hazard Powder Co., Mad-Hatter, Gleason's and a score of others. The decor of these places varies in detail but seems to stem from a set formula that combines Victorian bric-a-brac, Tiffany-type lamps, red checked tablecloths, and sawdust in an atmosphere loosely categorized as "Anglo-Irish." When first introduced in some of the older singles pubs, Friday's, Dr. Generosity, and Mad-Hatter, it reflected remarkable imagination and ingenuity on the part of the owners. Unfortunately, however, the pattern is a little too familiar today, but that in no way seems to affect the amazing popularity of these establishments.

Contrary to popular opinion, there is more than one variety of tavern on the upper east side. Lovers of the traditional frequent Daly's Dandelion, Martell's, P. J. Moriarty, and Willie's. Sports buffs and occasional celebrities congregate at Drake's Drum, the Kangaroo Pub, McMaster's, the Red Blazer, and Waltzing Matilda. Music lovers look to Mugg's, My House, Gregory's, and Patch's Inn. Finally, everyone on some occasion or another, visits the Plastic Gardens of Adam's Apple and enjoys the sheer extravagance of Maxwell's Plum, one of the most remarkable bar-restaurants in Manhattan.

ADAM'S APPLE

ADDRESS: 1117 First Ave. (at 61st St.); 371–8651
BAR HOURS: Noon–4 A.M.
FOOD: American (moderate)
CREDIT CARDS: AE BA CB DC MC
DRESS: Smart casual
SPECIAL FEATURES: Decor and people watching
LIVELIEST TIMES: 9 P.M.–3 A.M. Wed.–Fri.

It took a team of psychiatrists to come up with the ultimate in appealing decor for the singles crowd. After exhaustive, but presumably fascinating, research, they concluded that young, liberated individuals relish the garden atmosphere—the intimacy of vegetation-shrouded patios, the inviting temptations of an updated Garden of Eden.

It appears they were right, although Adam's Apple is perhaps not exactly what they had in mind. For this is a plastic Garden of Eden—not just a few prefabricated flowers mind you, but a literal forest of plastic trees, fruits and flora, with waterfalls, open fireplaces, Astroturf lawns, and the theme "don't resist temptation" appropriately represented by a juicy red apple with one large bite out of it.

There's an unusually relaxed atmosphere here (relaxed, that is, for a singles bar) even though the bar, dining rooms, and leafy glades are packed, particularly after 9 P.M. later in the week and the management had instituted some rather rigid policies. First, there's an age minimum: Women must be twenty-one, men twenty-three. No jeans are allowed and no sneakers. Wednesday, Friday, and Sunday nights there's a minimum of $6.00 per person after 9:30 P.M. But none of this seems to be limiting the crowd.

Two elevated dance floors start shaking at 10 P.M. every night. A disc jockey in a treehouse keeps the music coming. One of the dance floors is primarily for the upstairs dining room, which generally is reserved for couples who want to enjoy the atmosphere but escape the crowd downstairs.

Since its opening only three years ago, Adam's Apple has almost doubled in size, and every square inch is in active use—especially at the bar, where people often line up four and five deep. This kind of garden is obviously good therapy for an awful lot of patrons.

DALY'S DANDELION

ADDRESS: 1029 Third Ave. (at 61st St.); 838–0780
BAR HOURS: 11 A.M.–4 P.M.
FOOD: Hamburgers, etc. (moderate)
CREDIT CARDS: None
DRESS: Mixed
SPECIAL FEATURES: Porch dining

When Skitch Henderson bought Daly's about nine years ago, it was still a "short draw" bar: The beer kegs were rolled directly under the bar and tapped where they lay. Empty kegs were stored in the back room, and by the end of the evening, it looked like the site of a log-rolling contest.

Since the famous musician took over, he's eliminated that rather archaic and inconvenient tradition. But other than that, he's "tried to do things that wouldn't disturb her . . . for she's a grand lady." And indeed, Daly's is the "grand old lady of 61st Street," dating back to the early 1900s.

Mr. Henderson has polished and cleaned her a bit, and brought some original stained-glass signs up from out of the basement. He and his partner, George Cothran, have added dandelion-inspired wallpaper. The napkins and waiters' ties have the same design. And somehow, with a slightly fresh face, Daly's has been reborn. No longer a famous speakeasy or Tammany Hall meeting place, it now offers a home away from home for the man or woman who likes the feel of a comfortable saloon.

On his opening night nine years ago, Mr. Henderson had John Lindsay tending bar. And the place has been packed ever since. At lunch, ladies have their chauffeurs drive them to Daly's so they can be seen by others lunching there for the same purpose. But after lunch, New York's saloon-lovers start coming in, and around 6 P.M., when the businessmen pausing for a pre-subway sip, are gone, the real fans show up. Unescorted females feel safe here, and while they can meet single men, they often just sit around the bar or at the tables drinking and chatting late into the night. Mr. Henderson points out, however, that what often transpires during whispered conversations at the bar "makes showbusiness

221

look like the Presbyterian Church." But he dutifully adds that that's true of any place in New York City.

An enclosed promenade on two sides of Daly's shelters additional tables for people who like to watch the passing parade outside or who just want a little privacy.

Daly's has a lot of strength: its character and charm, the free-pour drinks, and the fact that single women feel comfortable here. The original Tiffany lamps (not the famous style, but others crafted by Tiffany), the slightly wobbly wooden chairs, the chipped tile floor, and the grand old bar herself all seem to represent a stability amidst nostalgia that is simply irresistible.

DON DENTON'S PUB

ADDRESS: 154 E. 79th St. (between Lexington and Third aves.);
744-9519
BAR HOURS: 11 A.M.–4 A.M.
FOOD: Mainly Italian (moderate)
CREDIT CARDS: None
DRESS: Informal
SPECIAL FEATURES: Backgammon
LIVELIEST TIMES: 10 P.M.–4 A.M. most evenings

If Alex Getzoff, winner of the 1974 Fort Lauderdale Backgammon Championship, or Don Denton himself, ever challenge you to a little backgammon at the pub's special tables, beware. Unless you consider yourself something of an expert or are independently wealthy, it may be better to remain an observer from the bar and spend time matching wits and repartee with barman Alvin Shapiro.

Decor in this small but pleasant haven of good fellowship is totally unremarkable, and while the Italian cuisine (prepared by a chef that Don managed to steal away from the San Remo) is unusually good, it's not what seems to attract the pub's unique collection of regulars. Don claims that "forty percent of my customers have a pile of money and don't work" (he seems to include himself in that category). Pop in any late evening toward the end of the week and you'll find young debutantes, members of the nouveau and not-so-nouveau-riche, celebrities, occasional segments of the Onassis clan, backgammon freaks, and even Harold—Don's enormous (and we mean enormous!) Great Dane. It's certainly a change from the heavy neighborhood singles scene.

DRAKE'S DRUM

ADDRESS: 1629 Second Ave. (between 84th and 85th sts.);
988–2826
BAR HOURS: 11 A.M.–4 A.M.
FOOD: American (inexpensive)
CREDIT CARDS: None
DRESS: Very casual
SPECIAL FEATURES: Free lunchtime hamburger with $1 drink,
Whitbread on tap, Sun. brunch noon–4 P.M.
LIVELIEST TIMES: 9 P.M.–2 A.M. Tues.–Sat.

Now here's a British-flavored pub that has some real authenticity. Not only is owner Jimmy Duke a true Liverpudlian with a
wry sense of humor, but his barmen are British and so are many

224

of his customers. The crowd is young and the place is popular with the less aggressive singles. Jimmy doesn't like hassling and is not above showing the door to overpossessive Romeos. As a result, the nights we were there we saw numerous women dining together in undisturbed peace.

The decor is familiar although the great Union Jack hanging between the rafters and the fine original seascapes give it added atmosphere—a slightly nautical flavor also reflected in old bells, anchors, and winching ropes.

Although Drake's Drum is not such a pronounced sports bar as the RED BLAZER, it's popular with local rugby teams in particular, and the TV is always on for major sporting events. Strangely, darts never really caught on here. But Jimmy Duke is proud of his tennis and softball teams and claims that his bar has developed a reputation with worldwide sports fans as an "international locale." On a recent visit to Copenhagen he even met an Indian jewelry merchant wearing a Drakes Drum T-shirt.

Another notable feature—the bar area is separated from the dining tables by a low partition, so there's plenty of room for serious elbow-bending in the evenings when the place really moves.

DR. GENEROSITY

ADDRESS: 1403 Second Ave. (at 73rd St.); 861–2230
BAR HOURS: 3 P.M.–4 A.M.
FOOD: Mainly American (inexpensive)
CREDIT CARDS: None
DRESS: Casual
SPECIAL FEATURES: Poetry readings Sat. 2 P.M.–4 P.M., "Inflation Specials" most evenings 6 P.M.–8 P.M., $2 minimum on Fri. and Sat., "Jam Sessions" 10:30 P.M.–2 A.M. Sun. and Mon.
LIVELIEST TIMES: 9 P.M.–4 A.M. Wed. and weekends

Along with a handful of other singles establishments in the area, Dr. Generosity is truly a legend in its own time. It has a special magic that comes from a subtle blend of the right people,

the right atmosphere, the right decor—and the right management. Maybe the size helps, too; it's small. Each of the spaces and niches has its own distinct character. For our tastes, there are times when it seems a little too small, but that doesn't appear to bother the young crowd who arrive in waves nightly—late at night usually—although the 6 P.M.–8 P.M. "inflation special" dinners have generated an earlier and equally devoted following.

Decor is a kind of random-funk complete with battered piano, softball trophies, posters of rock stars, a rack of the latest issues of the *Village Voice*, photographs of theatrical and showbiz personalities, and copies of the "Desiderata" which appear to be everywhere including on the back of the menu.

Yet all this is not new. Admittedly when David McSheehey "designed" the place in 1969 it was considered slightly daring.

Initial reactions varied from the "Way out man" response to more conservative views. "Who the heck wants to spend the evening in an attic full of junk?" Apparently most people in the neighborhood did. The concept caught on and has been used ad nauseam throughout Manhattan.

But Dr. Generosity remains a special place. It still has the Saturday poetry readings and continues to release anthologies published by the Dr. Generosity Press. Also on Sunday and Monday nights (10:30 P.M.–2 A.M.) there's the jam session that in the past has featured such celebrities as Richie Havens and Odetta—and continues to offer an excellent selection of jazz, folk, blues, and rock music.

In recent years the clientele has changed a little. There's been a decline in the overheavy singles scene, and the place has started to attract a more sophisticated and older group. One of the bartenders describes the scene as "neighborhood, except that our neighborhood is worldwide." He could be right.

FRIDAY'S

ADDRESS: 1152 First Ave. (at 63rd St.); 832–8512
BAR HOURS: Noon–4 A.M. daily
FOOD: American/hamburgers (inexpensive)
CREDIT CARDS: None
DRESS: Very casual
SPECIAL FEATURES: Weekend brunch, the "Hugely Famous" hamburger
LIVELIEST TIMES: 8 P.M.–2 A.M. most evenings

Richard Liss, once a dean of discipline at a public school, and now manager of Friday's, claims that 63rd Street and First Avenue is the best girl-watching corner in the city. He may well be right, but we were far too busy watching the young and beautiful at play inside Friday's to cast more than a casual glance outside.

Friday's, or to give the correct title T.G.I. (Thank God It's . . .) Friday's, is a landmark on the Manhattan singles scene. It

227

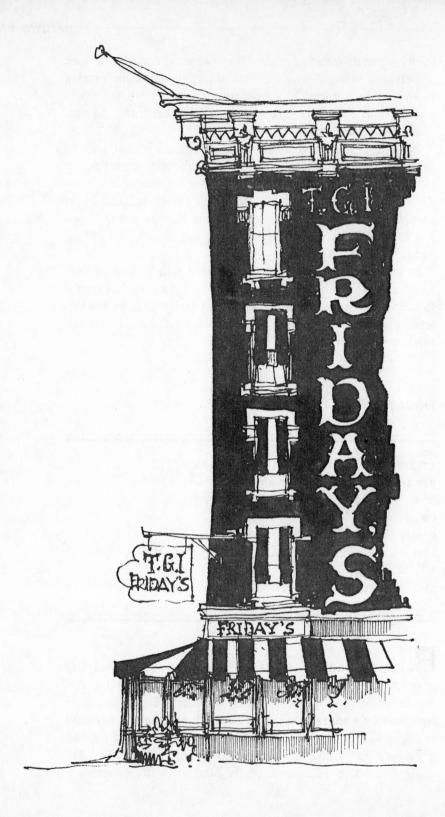

opened in 1965, around the same time as MAXWELL'S PLUM, and is still one of the most popular spots in the "meat rack" zone—even though its decadent-Victorian decor (Tiffany-type shades, old carved bar, Hemingway fans, and potted palms) has been imitated a hundred or more times in bars all over the city.

The atmosphere is perhaps a little more restrained than in the old party days when gorilla-suited employees would bound across First Avenue stopping cars and literally drag their occupants in for the revelries, or when horse-drawn chariots complete with Ben Hurs would reenact the famous chariot race sequence around the block. But there's still life in the old place yet . . . and plenty of it! The music, bass-heavy, blasts out of the jukebox and the place is packed almost every evening. However, if the music stops, says Mr. Liss, the place becomes an instant morgue. Conversation falters and customers look around uncomfortably until someone relieves the tension with a quarter.

In addition to the standard singles crowd (twenty to thirty years old), Friday's is beginning to attract an older group of singles and divorcées. It's also become the in place this year (month, week, day???) for stewardesses. So much so, that the area has been labelled—a little unkindly—the stew-zoo.

Alan Stillman, Ben Benson, and Ernest Kalman, the owners of Friday's (also, TUESDAY'S, WEDNESDAY'S, and THURSDAY'S), are still confused over the success of the place. All they know is that they have been responsible for about 1,000 marriages—and 3,000 divorces!! However, in accordance with the old adage, "Don't knock success," they've started up ten more Fridays' in such places as Dallas, Nashville, Atlanta, and Houston, and they're all booming.

One of the most attractive features here is the sidewalk porch where the Beautiful People sit munching on hamburgers and sipping from huge goblets of cream-topped Irish coffee. Unfortunately, Friday's ice cream parlor, Sunday's, which used to be located just off First Avenue, has recently been closed to make room for internal expansion.

If you're not familiar with the singles scene, Friday's is a good place for initiation into the subtleties of the game. On the other hand, if you're an old regular, you've probably not even read this far because you already know about Friday's.

GOBBLER'S KNOB

ADDRESS: 1461 First Ave. (at 76th St.); 249–0004
BAR HOURS: Noon–4 A.M.
FOOD: American and European (moderate)
CREDIT CARDS: AE MC
DRESS: Casual
SPECIAL FEATURES: Live music, brunch with classical music, cocktail hour with hot hors d'oeuvres 4 P.M.–7 P.M.
LIVELIEST TIMES: 9 P.M.–4 A.M. Wed.–Fri.

How's this for a combination—classical music in a pubby setting with continental cuisine run by the charming ex-wife of a famous Knicks player and a name with most unfortunately British (and unladylike) connotations!

Barbara Heyman has been associated with this delightful place for more than six years and recently took over from her husband, Art Heyman, when he went off to open OPUS I (48th Street between First and Second avenues)—an unusual combination of discotheque with backgammon tables and tennis courts.

A while back this was the Bishop's Purse, well known for its cuisine and its menus bound into voluminous law books. The tradition remains. The food is good (particularly the duck—the chef came from the Duck Joint restaurant), and menus are still bound in books, although the subject matter tends to be a little lighter.

The bar, which attracts a strong sports crowd and mature singles, is pleasantly separated from the dining rooms and has a late-night scene. Barbara is usually around and has developed the knack of creating an intimate clubby atmosphere. First-timers at the place are made most welcome. If they look a little lost, Barbara will select from her bevy of friends and make appropriate introductions. Needless to say, first-timers soon become regulars.

The recent introduction of live classical music (usually limited to flute and piano) 8 P.M.–midnight on Thursdays and during Saturday and Sunday brunch has drawn considerable publicity. It's an excellent idea—and tastefully done. In fact Barbara has been so encouraged by the popularity of the Gobbler's live entertainment that she recently introduced "showcase" evenings each Monday for talented but little-known singers and musicians. Since Mondays are traditionally dull in this area, we welcome the idea.

THE KANGAROO PUB

ADDRESS: 1550 First Ave. (between 80th and 81st sts.); 744–9400
BAR HOURS: 4 P.M.–4 A.M. Mon.–Fri., noon–4 A.M. Sat. and Sun.
FOOD: None
CREDIT CARDS: None
DRESS: Casual
SPECIAL FEATURES: Darts, ladies' night on Mon. (free champagne and flowers)
LIVELIEST TIMES: 10 P.M.–2 A.M. Tues. and weekends

What a refreshing change! Kangaroo, owned by New Zealander Rod Dreyer and his wife, Carol, is a true neighborhood pub, and while it appeals to some of the younger singles in the area, it's a far different place from the heavy meat rack bars nearby.

It's always so full of life. On a midweek evening you'll find some of Manhattan's finest darts players at the two boards (Tuesdays are the big tournament nights), and couples at tables playing Kalah—a complex African game with overtones of chess and backgammon. Burly members of the New York rugby club may also be lined up along the bar. But if they're in a celebrating mood, Carol usually pushes them into a special room at the back where they can sprawl on old sofas and sing those notorious rugby songs without alarming the gentler folk out front. By the way, if you have no idea what rugby football is all about, take a look at the posters in this back room; they explain the rules and characteristics of this rigorous but gentlemanly sport.

Kangaroo, originally known as the Crooked Fence, has been around for almost six years. It used to feature showcase acts on

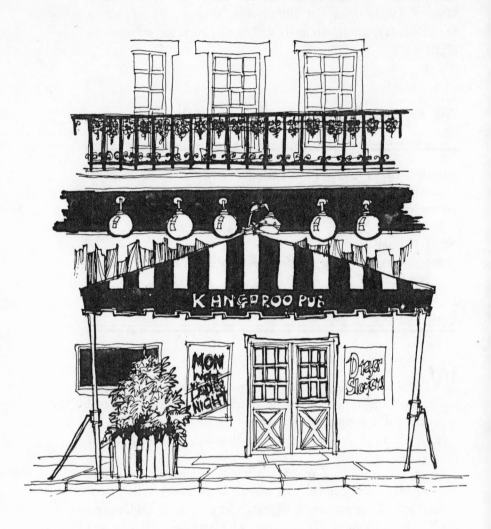

a small stage, and live rock music on certain evenings. However, the showcase talent has been transferred to CATCH A RISING STAR across the street.

In addition to Foster's Australian Lager, Kangaroo offers its own notorious cocktail, the Kiwi Kicker (Southern Comfort, 151-proof rum, juices, and grenadine), which normally becomes the victory drink whenever the pub's female darts team (Dreyer's Slayers) win a major match. And if the rugby boys happen to be there at the same time—the Kangaroo really starts kicking.

THE MAD HATTER (of Second Avenue)

ADDRESS: 1485 Second Ave. (at 77th St.); 628–4917
BAR HOURS: Noon–4 A.M.
FOOD: Steaks and hamburgers
CREDIT CARDS: None
DRESS: Casual
SPECIAL FEATURES: Monday "chicken" night
LIVELIEST TIMES: 9 P.M.–3 A.M. Thurs.–Sat.

Here's one of the original singles bars in this part of town. The familiar sawdust, old beams, and trinket-laden atmosphere has a real thrown-together look. And according to owners Dan Sweeney and John Barnes that's pretty much the way it happened. The transformation of the redoubtable old Murphy's into The Mad Hatter took about four days according to John!

For weeks the place had no name—that is until one of the cooks started hanging a few old hats from the rafters. Then everyone started bringing in headgear until today there's a veritable museum up there in the dust: stetsons, derbies, sombreros, top hats, helmets, coolie hats—the lot!

It's worth exploring the bric-a-brac in this Irish/English-flavored pub. Note the enormous steins over the bar. They're not just part of the decor—patrons can, and often do, order them filled with frothing beer. Even a thirsty rugby team could make the $15 Papa Bear stein last most of the night. And talking about rugby, the Mad Hatter occasionally becomes a clubhouse for the New York teams—there's even a special basement room for their exclusive use when their song sessions get too raucous for the customers.

Some of the staff here also are members of the rugby team featured in Richard Harris' film *The Molly Maquires,* and the scoreboard used in the movie hangs near the bar.

During the winter, this is a big ski-scene center. Groups meet here on Friday evenings prior to setting off to Hunters, and Dan Sweeney occasionally shows his ski movies on a screen near the door. To complete the picture we should also mention that the Mad Hatter has its own softball team.

233

Somehow the staff also finds time to serve the crowds of young couples and singles who throng the place, particularly late in the week. The food is limited in range but well prepared, and the "all you can eat" Monday chicken dinner is a true bargain.

MARTELL'S

ADDRESS: 1469 Third Ave. (at 83rd St.); UN 1–6110
BAR HOURS: Noon–2 A.M. Sun.–Thurs., noon–4 A.M. Fri. and
 3 A.M. Sat.
FOOD: American and European (moderate)
CREDIT CARDS: AE BA DC MC
DRESS: Casual but mixed
SPECIAL FEATURES: Old-fashioned ambience and interesting
 crowd
LIVELIEST TIMES: 7 P.M.–midnight Wed.–Sat.

You can feel the history here. Little has been done to the place since it began as Kaiser's, a true Yorkville bar catering to a predominantly German population. The dark panelled walls, white

tiled floor, old fireplaces, and elaborate wooden screen separating the bar from one of the dining areas, have all been retained and treasured. During prohibition, Kaiser's was a cozy little speakeasy. The tailor next door loaned a few of his dummies to fill in window space, and the main entrance was off a small door at the side of the building. Some of the old secret switches, knobs, bells, and buttons still remain and were actively used by curious customers until owner Ralph Martell recently disconnected the whole system to preserve his sanity.

In the early sixties Martell's was one of the main singles bars in the neighborhood. However, the emergence of FRIDAY'S, the MAD HATTER, and a score of similar establishments left Martell's with a more mature and mixed crowd of theatre and TV people, Wall-Streeters, and local professionals. While singles still meet here, it's also the kind of place where women can relax over a drink and a magazine (there are a score of latest issues hanging by the bar) without hassle. The same goes for "stars" and "superstars." Although the walls are crammed with photos of beaming celebrities enjoying the ambience of the bar, on one of the days we visited John Lennon and Paul McCartney had just completed dinner without a single request for an autograph!

A few years ago Ralph expanded his dining area into the adjacent building and personally designed the room, with its vast fireplace, a rack of old kitchen pans, and brick walls. It's a charming place for dinner served under the watchful eye of Sigmund, Ralph's Austrian manager.

MAXWELL'S PLUM

ADDRESS: 1181 First Avenue (at 64th St.); 628–2100
BAR HOURS: Noon–2:30 A. M.
FOOD: European and American (expensive)
CREDIT CARDS: AE BA CB DC MC
DRESS: Mixed
SPECIAL FEATURES: Fine cuisine, atmosphere, and decor
LIVELIEST TIMES: After 8 P.M. most evenings

From the outside, this most renowned of upper east side establishments looks about ready for the wrecker's ball. Its single-story, mud colored walls, and a roof littered with vents and air conditioners, hardly seem appropriate to its reputation. However, inside is another world—the result of one wealthy man's totally abandoned indulgence in an incredibly eclectic love for art. It's a place that must be taken in inch by inch, for the visual impact of the whole is so overwhelming, and owner Warner Leroy (son of movie producer Mervyn Leroy), is still collecting additional pieces in Europe.

Sitting at the enormous center bar, you can get most of the view. Start with the superb ceramic figures and animals hanging from the ceiling over the glass-enclosed café running along the two sides of Maxwell's. Then focus on the ceilings themselves. Traditional tin covers a small area, but hand-stamped copper graces the major part and even runs down the walls. Notice the bright and beautiful lamps—newly designed—but made with original Tiffany glass. Over in the back room (where dining is in the French tradition with real silver and a host of tuxedoed waiters) there's a gigantic rear-lit ceiling made from thousands of tiny pieces of the same kind of Tiffany glass. Fresh flowers abound, and a florist comes in daily to arrange the floral decorations on the individual dining tables. Along the rear wall of this back room is also a huge mirror with a magnificent hand-carved frame, created by Paul Moses, whose genius also inspired the central bar.

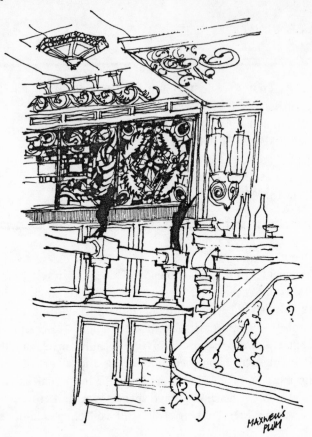

MAXWELL'S
PLUM

The restaurant's wine list goes from the sublime to the ridiculously sublime, and there's a special selection that must be ordered twenty-four hours in advance to enable proper decanting. Altogether there are more than 60,000 bottles in the Plum's cellars.

The clientele is as diversified as the décor. During the day the central bar is relatively tranquil with a gentle flow of well-dressed, unhurried patrons. However, during the later evenings, the change is dramatic, and by 10 P.M. the crush at the bar is incredible. Diners leaving the sedate back room stare in amazement at that solid block of bodies in the middle of the room—a startling example of the intensity of the Manhattan singles scene.

If you'd rather avoid this unusual phenomenon, stop by for a drink or something to eat in the afternoon. (The master chef formerly worked for Charles de Gaulle.) The luncheon prices are reasonable and you'll be able to linger over your drink while feasting visually on the decor.

McMASTER'S

ADDRESS: 413 71st St. (between York and First aves.); 744–1447
BAR HOURS: 11:30 A.M.–4 A.M.
FOOD: American with occasional Chinese dishes (moderate)
CREDIT CARDS: AE DC MC
DRESS: Smart informal
SPECIAL FEATURES: Garden patio, sporting crowd
LIVELIEST TIMES: 10 P.M.–4 A.M. most evenings

Dorie McMaster's somewhat turbulent career in the New York bar business finally seems to have settled down. At last she has her own place (nicknamed "Dorie's Last Pop Stand" by her friends) in what used to be Yesterday's Hutch, a bar once popular with the beer and darts crowd. All that remains of the old scene is the gigantic air conditioner over the door, big enough to service a department store.

The pleasant, carpeted drinking area now has dark walls and photographs of renowned sporting celebrities. In fact on the busier week nights, the bar becomes a veritable "who's who" in the game business—stars of the Jets, the Giants, the Yankees ("my Yankees" as Dorie calls them), the Islanders, the Knicks, and the Mets all seem to regard this as their own exclusive domain and Dorie as their mascot. Take a look at the menu cover: It's Dorie's way of saying "Hello," "Thank you," and "I love you" to all her many friends.

Past the attractive green and white dining room is one of the quaintest patios in this part of town. On a summer evening the overhanging trees, waterfalls, spotlights, and barbecue provide an almost Californian atmosphere, although unfortunately Dorie hasn't found room for a pool yet. The food, consisting mainly of steaks, chicken, and seafood dishes, is well-prepared by the Chinese chef, and the restaurant attracts as devoted a following as the bar itself.

MUGG'S

ADDRESS: 1134 First Ave. (between 62nd and 63rd sts.); 838–7050

BAR HOURS: 11:30 A.M.–1 A.M. Sun.–Thurs., noon–2 A.M. Fri. and Sat.

FOOD: American (inexpensive)

CREDIT CARDS: AE BA CB DC MC

DRESS: Casual

SPECIAL FEATURES: Sat. and Sun. champagne brunch, occasional live jazz (Min. $3.50 on weekends)

LIVELIEST TIMES: 8 P.M.–11 P.M. later in the week

Although the decor is familiar (old Victorian pub), Mugg's provides a little welcome relief on the fringe of the singles strip. While the place is by no means unknown to the younger crowd, it also appeals to a diversified clientele. Jerry Brodie, the owner, calls it a family place that attracts people "from the high chair to the wheel chair." The family image is certainly apt. Jerry's father-in-law (once a partner in the now defunct Jack Dempsey establishment on Times Square), his wife, his daughter, and two sons-in-law are all on the staff. Women seem to feel comfortable here. If there's any uninvited hassling Jerry is usually around to put a stop to it. After all, he explains, "this is my living room, and I like people to behave politely."

The menu features (at last count) twelve different varieties of hamburger as well as homemade soups, sirloin steak, ribs, and chicken. In addition to the porch area there's a pleasant dining room at the back, complete with red-check tablecloths and an unusual assortment of artwork—lithographs, posters, oil paintings, and caricatures.

Two new features have recently been introduced: 5 P.M.–7 P.M. every evening is Rebate Time (every third drink is on the house), and on Monday night there's a Twofer dinner—two for the price of one.

J. G. MELON

ADDRESS: 1291 Third Ave. (at 74th St.); RH 4–0585
BAR HOURS: 11 A.M.–4 A.M.
FOOD: Hamburgers, etc. (inexpensive)
CREDIT CARDS: None
DRESS: Mixed
SPECIAL FEATURES: People-watching, "melon" paintings
LIVELIEST TIMES: 7 P.M.–1 A.M. most evenings

Jack O'Neill, part owner of this delightful bar-restaurant, must be one of the few men in the world ever to have refused an original de Kooning. It was an occasion he'll never forget, and we're tempted to tell the story. However, Jack is a natural raconteur, so ask him about it instead.

Melon's is a relative newcomer to Third Avenue. Way back in the thirties the place was known as the Central Tavern, a neighborhood Irish bar run by two Italians. When Jack and his partner, George Mourges, took it over two years ago they decided the place needed a strong new image, so they borrowed the melon motif from Goldies (an old pub once on Second Avenue and now on Fire Island) and filled the place with paintings of melons in every conceivable art style, including a superb surrealist piece by Jackie Wilson that hangs over the center of the bar. The idea caught on. Even Frank Roth donated a linear abstract work that glows on the wall separating the bar from the rear dining room.

Melon's is an amazingly popular place. It's virtually institutionalized with the in-crowd in the same way that P. J. CLARKE'S dominates the mid-part of Third Avenue. It's not only popular with the Onassis clan (they really move around) but has a distinct following with the literary, theatrical, and film crowds. And the bar is not the only feature attracting the patronage. The food, which is just about as basic as you could find in New York—hamburgers, chili, and omelettes—has an astounding reputation (we vouch for that), and customers regularly have to wait more than an hour to grab a tiny table in the even tinier dining area.

241

If you have problems getting into Melon's, there are a couple of adjoining places worthy of attention. For the singles crowd, Churchill's is a small, very friendly place that features Watney's draft in a British pub setting complete with large photographs of the "old bulldog." Allen's, a little farther down the avenue, is predominantly a restaurant but has an old-fashioned charm and a long history. Even Jack O'Neill recommends this place and he should know; he worked there for many years before establishing Melon's.

PATCH'S INN

ADDRESS: 314 E. 70th St. (between First and Second aves.);
879–4220
BAR HOURS: 5 P.M.–2 A.M.; closed Mon.
FOOD: American and European (moderate)
CREDIT CARDS: AE BA MC
DRESS: Informal
SPECIAL FEATURES: Live music every night (dixieland Wed. 8
P.M.–midnight, Sun. 6 P.M.–10 P.M., $3 minimum with jazz
LIVELIEST TIMES: 8 P.M.–midnight Tues., Wed., and Sun.

What a joyous transformation—an old Czech social club near the heart of Yorkville becomes one of the liveliest and most attractive bar-restaurants in the neighborhood. As its name and the design of its matchbook covers might suggest, the patchwork quilt theme has been carried to its exotic extreme. The walls around the bar are covered in large squares of bright contrasting materials, table cloths are all hand-sewn quilts, and in the delightful rear dining area, which comes complete with fireplace and huge chandelier, are two exquisite Tomas Stephens quilt tapestries. Scattered throughout are vases of fresh country flowers, pine cones, and dried corn cobs. It's an atmosphere reminiscent of country farms, grandparents, and simple, time-honored crafts. More important though—it's fun. The food, which is a little more exotic than that which grandma might have prepared, is excellent. And owner Phil Lendino proudly hands out printed recipes for Patch's shrimp in ale batter (once featured on the *Eyewitness News* program) to his invariably beaming customers.

The dixieland jazz is topflight (Wednesday and Sunday). However if you're looking for something a little less raucous, there's a pianist and singer on Thursdays, Fridays, and Saturdays and special guests on Tuesdays (call for details).

P. J. MORIARTY

ADDRESS: 1034 Third Ave. (at 61st St.); TE 8–4688
BAR HOURS: Noon–midnight
FOOD: American/European (moderate)
CREDIT CARDS: AE BA CB DC MC
DRESS: Casual
LIVELIEST TIMES: 7 P.M.–10 P.M. Wed.–Fri.

This area of town is famous for its "P. J.'s" (O'Hara's, CLARKE's, and MORIARTY's) and to add to the confusion, there are actually three separate P. J. Moriarty's in the city. However, this particular one with its dark cedar paneling, old beer pumps, and Tiffany lamps (two originals) is our favorite. The Old Third Avenue El once used to trundle past the bar, and in a flush of

nostalgia Mr. Moriarty not only covered the walls with old El photographs, but even runs a scale model of the train and two carriages along the walls above the bar.

Unlike many of the more boisterous Third Avenue places, P. J. Moriarty's has a quiet, almost clublike calm, except in the early evenings when the two-drinks-and-then-home crowd takes over. After that the restaurant comes into its own, serving an interesting selection of American and European dishes.

This is definitely not a singles spot. On the other hand, if you need a change of pace and a relaxed drink in nostalgic surroundings, P. J. Moriarty's is your place.

THE RECOVERY ROOM

ADDRESS: 417 E. 70th St. (between First and York aves.); 628–3724
BAR HOURS: 11:30 A.M.–4 A.M.
FOOD: American/European (moderate)
CREDIT CARDS: Pending
DRESS: Casual
LIVELIEST TIMES: After 10 P.M. most evenings

The Recovery Room, located on a quiet stretch of 70th Street that still retains some of the old character of Yorkville, has gone through many recent changes. Its dark, shuttered facade has been replaced by contemporary bronzed-aluminum panels, the tiny front bar area has been extended to provide an Italian-styled dining room, and an additional similar expansion is planned in the near future. Even the intravenous bottles above the bar, which once were used as juice dispensers, have been removed.

Nevertheless, the bar scene is still active and particularly popular after 10 P.M. most evenings with singles and the nursing crowd from the nearby hospitals. During the early evening the dining room tends to dominate; and the food, for such a small place, is excellent. Particularly popular dishes include veal Zürichoise, pork chop Ville Mar, duckling Beauregarde, and bass duclère.

245

The managers and barmen are all old maestros of the singles scene: Eddie Hart was manager at FRIDAY'S for five years; Buddy Devaney once owned The Ugly Ostrich, and Marvin Cohen came from the Bum Steer.

It's a warm, friendly place and the hospital crowd gives it a particularly clubby atmosphere.

THE RED BLAZER

ADDRESS: 1571 Second Ave. (between 81st & 82nd sts.); 535-0847
BAR HOURS: 4 P.M.–4 A.M. Mon.–Fri., noon–4 A.M. Sat. and Sun.
FOOD: American (inexpensive)
CREDIT CARDS: "The Red Blazer" card only!
DRESS: Casual
SPECIAL FEATURES: Sat. and Sun. brunch noon–4 P.M.
LIVELIEST TIMES: 10 P.M.–3 A.M. weekends

This is one of New York's best-known sports bars—a favorite with team members of the Islanders and the Yankees. Three television sets cover every major sporting event, and Denis Carey, the owner, claims his bar was the first in New York to install cable TV for special sports features not covered on the normal channels.

Ironically the Red Blazer attracts, in addition to its regular clientele of stocky athletics addicts, two unusual fringe groups. The first is an enthusiastic contingent of females who come, not to mingle with the burlies at the bar, but to watch major hockey events. The second is the Wall Street crowd attracted both by the atmosphere of the place and its inexpensive but generously served prime ribs, steaks, and seafood. Such is the Red Blazer's reputation with the downtown sophisticates that they renamed it La Blazer Rouge and persuaded Denis to issue special credit cards for the place.

The sawdust floors, stained glass, Tiffany lamps, and cartwheels-on-the-wall décor are familiar but pleasant. Friday nights particularly attract a sizeable singles crowd, but the real spirit of the place comes from the sports lovers who regard the bar as their second living room.

WALTZING MATILDA

ADDRESS: 1567 Second Ave. (between 81st and 82nd sts.); 744–9206
BAR HOURS: 11 A.M.–4 A.M.
FOOD: Limited American menu (inexpensive)
CREDIT CARDS: None
DRESS: Very casual
SPECIAL FEATURES: Good selection of English and Australian beers
LIVELIEST TIMES: 7 P.M.–11 P.M. Tues. and 9 P.M.–2 A.M. Fri.

This delightful little bar seems to be as well known in Kangaroo Alley (Earl's Court, London) as it is in Manhattan, and it's one of the first places that visiting Australians and Britishers make for once they hit the Big Apple. Doubtless the British tap beers (Watney's and Whitbread) and such famous down-under brews as Swan and Foster's are a feature attraction. But Waltzing Matilda is equally known for its excellent darts teams, one of which recently carried away the four-man team trophy at the Schmidts American Open Tournament in Philadelphia.

The place has only been around for a couple of years. Previously it was a rather notorious young hippy hang-out known as Bogeys, but owner Gino Reardon and friends gutted and refurbished it in a pleasant contemporary style slightly reminiscent of 162 SPRING STREET.

In addition to the pub's darts teams with names like The Koalas, Wallabies, and Kookaboros, there's also a rugby team— the Old Blues. Gino warns the uninitiated to avoid the nights when team members gather at Waltzing Matilda's—it gets a little raucous.

247

While the bar is not exactly a singles place, the crowd is young (twenty-five to thirty-five), and it's popular with some of the better-known rock artists—Alice Cooper, Spencer Davis, and Harry Nilsson. Tuesday night is darts night, so if you consider yourself a bit of an expert, join the real professionals in the basement.

WILLIE'S

ADDRESS: 1426 Third Ave. (at 81st St.); RH 4–9948
BAR HOURS: 11:30 A.M.–4 A.M.
FOOD: American and Chinese menu (inexpensive)
CREDIT CARDS: None
DRESS: Casual
SPECIAL FEATURES: Carlsberg on tap
LIVELIEST TIMES: Weekends from 10 P.M.

Moe Morrison, bartender and brother of owner Willie Morrison, describes this place as a "real tavern." We agree, and quite frankly, we were relieved to find a regular, old-fashioned watering hole in an area increasingly inundated with "instant-pub" and "disco-deli" establishments.

There's a spirit of permanency in Willie's that comes partly from the simple decor of the place (long bar, wooden booths, big TV for sporting events) but perhaps more significantly from the clientele, most of whom are daily regulars. Although the popular outdoor café area and bright posters and paintings on the walls suggest Willie is not averse to a young and cosmopolitan clientele, it's the club-like atmosphere of old friendships that gives the place its true character.

This spirit was evidenced a few years ago when a fire in the bar just prior to New Year's Eve left the place in a shambles. Willie called up all his regular patrons and told them he had no intention of closing the place for repairs. Within two hours forty loyal customers arrived in old clothes and proceeded to work all through the day and night, cleaning and rebuilding the interior. The following evening—New Year's Eve—Willie was back in

business and the bar had one of the biggest celebrations ever seen along this stretch of Third Avenue.

Another event was equally significant. On the bar's first anniversary night the regulars planned a celebration for Willie, who before he took over the place was well known on the east side as a "good guy" and a remarkable drinker. Together they collected over $700 and brought in a truck equipped with spotlights and a pink painted elephant. It was a fantastic night. The elephant ate over thirty pounds of peanuts, shook trunks with everyone in the bar, joined most of the partons in a drink, and left, a little unsteadily, early the following morning.

In contrast to these somewhat hectic occasions, Willie's is a relatively quiet place. The dining area is separated from the bar by a low screen and features an interesting menu of American dishes. If you desire something a little more exotic, there's a short list of Chinese dishes (chalked on a board behind the TV set) prepared by Willie's Chinese chef. We can recommend all of them.

and for
your further enjoyment...

BRANDY'S I

235 E. 84th St. (between Second and Third aves.); RH 4–9089

Over the years this grubby little pub with its sloping floors beams, posters, and even a yellow plastic bucket hung near the ceiling where the pipe leaks, has become one of the most popular late-night singles spots in the area. It's conducive to relaxed, intimate conversation at the small tables surrounding an even smaller stage on which folk singers perform regularly. Early evenings used to be quiet until owner Don Philistine introduced his 5 P.M.–9 P.M. Monday binge (all the steamed clams and mussels you can manage for $1.10) and his 6 P.M.–7 P.M. Wednesday evening cocktail party (free drinks—but you buy first).

CATCH A RISING STAR

1487 First Ave. (at 78th St.) ; 734-9777

Here's a rather unique institution. Rick Newman opened it a little while back as a modest showcase for young talent—singers, comedians, jugglers, magicians, and even animal acts. Thanks to considerable media publicity and Rick's incredible nose for talent, it's now a remarkably popular place, particularly during late evenings. Of course Rick's tastes don't always match those of the audience as the sign by the stage might suggest—"All entertainers must leave the stage instantly any objects are thrown."

Shows in the back area usually begin around 10 P.M., and there's a small minimum—$3 on weekdays, $5 Friday and Saturday. Come early and sit at the small front bar. The decor is all theatre—posters, photographs of successful artists, and various bits and pieces of Victorian memorabilia—and the crowd is young and lively.

ELAINE'S

1703 Second Ave. (at 88th St.); TE 1–9558

To anyone who knows anything about New York's bars, Elaine's is truly a landmark—a haven for the great names in America's literary, art, and film world. It's a small, dimly lit enclave of the cultured. Fine lithographs, posters, and paintings fill the walls near the bar, and the rear dining area is surrounded by an aged fresco illuminated by small lamps. A list of the regulars who come to enjoy Elaine's Italian cuisine would read like an international "Who's Who."

While its history could fill a book, Elaine's seems to have lost a little of its old charm. The reason is hard to define. Everything looks the same, it's always packed, but something's gone wrong according to many of those who know the place well. While we were there, Elaine Kaufman, who admittedly is known as a character, was bawling out the barman, cursing the waiters, and making threatening gestures at the kitchen staff. The only creature she seemed to smile at was her little pet terrier. However that's typical Elaine and that's what draws many of her clients. We only hope the place regains its old reputation. It's too good to fade.

FINNEGAN'S WAKE

1361 First Ave. (at 73rd St.); 737–3664

As you might expect from the name, this is another popular pub in the English/Irish tradition—but the décor is restrained. We found the lack of sawdust and bric-a-brac dangling from dusty ceilings most refreshing.

Late week nights tend to be liveliest and attract a mixed crowd of local medicos, older singles, and British-accented gentlemen. Tuesday evenings are usually given over to darts tournaments, and when the Finn's Wake team and followers are in a winning mood, anything can happen here. A while back there used to be live folk music sessions but they've been abandoned. It's a shame —they used to be fun.

FLANAGAN'S

1215 First Ave. (between 65th and 66th sts.); 472–0300

Originally known as Sullivan's, this is now a cheery Irish pub complete with brogued Irish waitresses (if you're lucky) and old English dishes—shepherd's pie, steak and kidney pie, and fish and chips. Like most bars in the area it livens up at night, although the crowd is more diversified than normally found in the singles places along the strip. Décor is standard Irish revival— beams, stained glass, and old lampshades. One special feature is worthy of note—most nights of the week there's live Irish music from 9 P.M. onwards. Unfortunately, dancing is discouraged; so grab a glass of Guinness and join in the choruses instead.

GLEASON'S TAVERN

1414 York Ave. (at 75th St.); 535-8702

Late-night scene—very dark, very singles, very crushed, and very popular. There's no point in describing the decor: First, it's totally irrelevant to the scene, and second, it's hard to stand far enough away from the melée to appreciate it.

Gleason's was one of the first bars in the city to attract a predominantly singles crowd and has outlived a score of imitators. It's a little too heavy for our tastes, but we're sure that won't worry Joe Gleason. He'll just keep on smiling to himself in the gloom.

For those seeking a slightly easier scene there's another Gleason's nearby at 1267 First Avenue; but somehow it lacks the spirit of the first.

GREGORY'S

1149 First Ave. (at 63rd St.); 371-2220

We're a little apprehensive about drawing too much attention to this one-time hamburger stand. It's perfect, yet so small that we'd hate to spoil it for the groups of devoted regulars who come here most evenings to listen to some of the best jazz in town. Pianist Brooks Kerr is one of the main attractions along with Russell Procope and drummer Sonny Greer, who worked with Duke Ellington for almost thirty years. A more recent addition is the Lee Konitz Trio (Mondays and Tuesdays) and we spent a delightful evening listening to Warren Chaisson, a sensitive vibes player, once with the George Shearing group.

255

With the exception of a few old instruments dangling from the rafters, décor is non-existant—and unnecessary. If it wasn't for the tiny porch addition, there'd hardly be room for more than a piano and a couple of patrons—standing.

For an unusual evening in this part of town, don't miss Gregory's. However, if you're not interested in jazz, leave it for those who are. There's a small cover charge—and it's worth every cent.

HARRY'S BACK EAST

1422 Third Ave. (at 81st St.); 249-6991

Harry's has almost become a classic in the city's gay bar scene. From its founding more than ten years ago it has developed a reputation as one of the friendliest places in town for the liberated male.

The owners, Gwen Saunders and Judy Trieste, take great pride in the bar's decor, which can only be described as accumulated bric-a-brac. In the dim half-light skeletons, masks, dusty teddy bears, theatrical hats, bottles, flags, cartwheels, air-inflated dolls, and a hundred other strange objects hang from the walls and ceiling. According to Lee Schwartz, who has been tending bar at Harry's for nine years, nothing is ever taken down. Whatever the customers put up, stays up. So if you've got an old candlestick, a couple of hubcaps, or a grandfather clock pendulum you don't happen to need, bring it along to Harry's and achieve a bit of instant immortality.

HOME

1748 Second Ave. (at 91st St.); 876-0744

This is another of our favorites, way up in the northern fringe of the upper east side. We're only giving it brief mention at this time because of planned major changes. Like the neighborhood itself, bristling with new high-rise apartments, Home is in a process of transformation. We plead, however, for retention of the random décor of farm implements, posters of rock artists, the excellent "good natural home cooking" menu (read the back— "an astrological view of Home"), and the unusual clientele of famous and not-so-famous rock artists, local construction workers, and singles with a generous smattering of eccentrics.

Where else in town could you enjoy a beer with Richie Havens, listen to live rock performances during the weekend, and listen to one of the bartenders plug his own record?

HUDSON BAY INN

1452 Second Ave. (at 76th St.); 861–5683

Decor is familiar except for overtones of the northern wilds of Canada in the form of snowshoes, wolfskins dangling from beams, and the unusually black interior reminiscent of dark winter days above the Arctic Circle. But somehow the spirit here is a little more friendly, a little less of a cruise bar than many of the adjoining places. The young people seem to know and like one another and it has that subtle club-feel that many of the more recently established places have yet to achieve.

257

J.P.'S

1471 First Ave. (between 76th and 77th sts.); 650–0804

It's questionable whether this place needs any more publicity. Every time we visited late at night the place was packed and not, as one might expect, with surging, seeking singles, but rather with people in or on the fringe of the music business—well-known rock stars, managers, agents, road men, and gaggles of groupies. And it's not a gawking, autograph-hunting place. It's more like a friendly club for people with similar interests and ambitions.

Jimmy Pullis, once a manager himself and close friend of James Taylor and Carly Simon, opened the place a little more than a year ago. It's already an established name in the area, not only because of the clientele but also the excellent seafood served here at dinnertime and the live, low-key folk and country music by top-flight artists (10 P.M.–2 A.M. Sunday and Monday).

Just a few additional notes if this seems your kind of place. It opens late (6 P.M.); the "scene" itself is much later (starting around 10 P.M.); there's a minimum at the tables—and, if you see a line of limousines outside, it possibly means J.P.'s is closed for one of its occasional press parties given by big names in the rock and folk world.

LION'S ROCK

316 E. 77th St. (between Second and Third aves.); 988–3610

Here's a relative newcomer worth watching. The long, narrow entrance corridor leads into a warm bar where the lion theme predominates—posters, caricatures, stuffed heads, and even a whole one just by the staircase to the lower dining room. But most impressive is the tiny outdoor patio behind which rises a great cliff of Manhattan rock—a true, lumpy slice of Lenox Hill.

It has an almost California feel to it—particularly the colored spots which highlight areas of the rock face. It's an unusual and imaginative little haven for the younger crowd.

MY HOUSE

1160 First Ave. (at 63rd St.); 832–9410

My House is strictly a night place. It's for the kind of people who don't want high-pressure hustling, who want to relax and enjoy a drink. It's a great change of pace for this frenetic neighborhood.

Owner Bob Saffir is proud of the customers he gets. They are more mature, they don't bother anyone, and they enjoy the jazz duo that plays Tuesday through Saturday.

There are two areas in the bar: "in front" and "in back." It is fairly private in the back area, and some people sit there to be away from the more spirited crowd up front. On Friday and Saturday nights there is a minimum charge: $4 per person up front and $3 "in back."

The interior of My House is tastefully done, with low ceilings and dim lights. It's conducive to conversation, possibly over Irish, French, or Jamaican coffee and is also a pleasant place for dining. (A full dinner menu, mainly American cuisine, is available.) However, there's no pressure to eat. All you have to do is relax and enjoy yourself.

PEDRO'S

251 E. 85th St. (at Second Ave.); UN 1–5020

You perhaps will wonder why we include this tiny vest-pocket pub in an area renowned for the quality of its more elaborate singles places. Well, for a start, the draft Spaten München and Stegmaier beer are good. But more than that, Pedro's attracts a strange combination of beer 'n' shot heavies and sophisticated jet-setters. Diamonds, denims, and derbies—all mixed up in a tiny room with smoke-stained bullfight posters and back-bar covered with hats of all shapes, sizes, and types.

You perhaps won't stay too long here, especially if there's no seat available (there are only fifteen)—but it's part of the neighborhood scene and the banana daquiris are superb.

SEPTEMBER'S

1442 First Ave. (at 75th St.); 861–4670

Here's one of the least pretentious of all singles places in the area. There's a porch café, some occasionally live music, a pub menu, and the odd Tiffany-type lamp—but that's about all. If you visit in the early evening you may wonder why the place stays in business. However, as with most singles spots in the neighborhood, the late-night scene is frantic—but friendly. Maybe that's what makes September's a little special. The crowd is young, lively, and open. Some of the heavier atmosphere of bars catering to older and often more anxious singles is refreshingly absent here. It's even worth the small admission charge (a relatively familiar characteristic of bars with a young clientele).

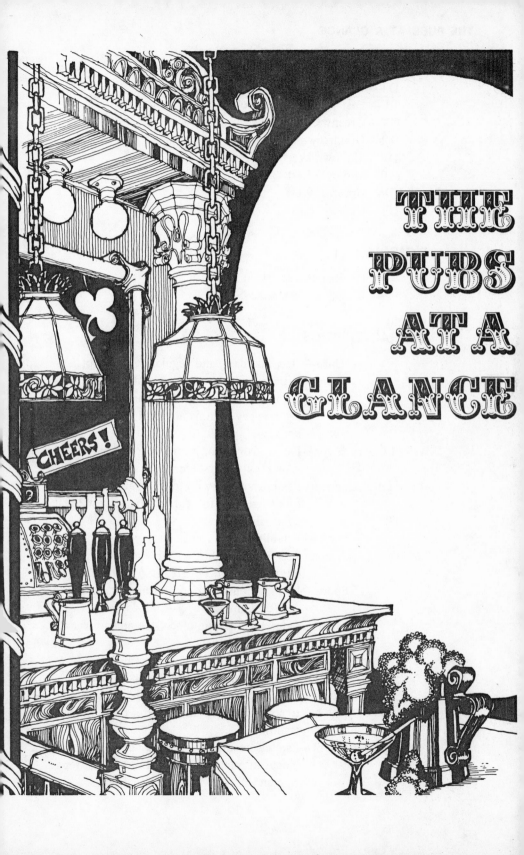

THE PUBS AT A GLANCE

ABBREVIATIONS

DT—Downtown
EV—East Village and Soho
GV—Greenwich Village
GR—Gramercy and Vicinity
MW—Midtown West and Chelsea
ME—Midtown East
UW—Uptown West
UE—Uptown East

SYMBOLS

•—Distinct characteristic
○—Partial characteristic

CHARACTERISTICS

Darts—Dart board (s) and regular tournaments.

Gay—Usually refers to male gay patrons, but does not imply exclusivity. Gay bars that discourage non-gay patrons are not included in this book.

Literary & Art—Patrons consist of journalists/writers/poets/artists/publishers, etc.

Live Entertainment—Establishments with piano bar, jazz band, folk singers, or full cabaret (usually without cover charge).

Singles—Establishments attracting young patrons (20–35) of both sexes who gather to pursue mutual romantic interests.

Sports—Patrons consisting of sporting personalities and/or admirers.

Students—Patrons consisting of college and university undergraduates.

Theatre—Patrons consisting of theatrical and "show biz" personalities and/or theatre-goers.

Traditional—Long-established bars with distinct and relatively unchanged atmosphere, clientele, and traditions.

Large Restaurant—Establishments offering a comprehensive menu, in relatively large dining areas, separate and distinct from the bar itself.

AREA	NAME & LOCATION	CHARACTERISTICS										PAGE NO.
		DARTS	GAY	LIT & ART	LIVE ENT.	SINGLES	SPORTS	STUDENTS	THEATER	TRADIT.	LARGE REST.	
UW	The Abbey Pub 237 W. 105th St. (at Broadway)	●		○		○		●	○			190
GR	The Abbey Tavern 354 Third Ave. (at 26th St.)					●					●	91
GV	Adam & Eve Waverly Pl. (at Mercer St.)					●		●			●	79
UE	Adam's Apple 1117 First Ave. (at 61st St.)					●		●			●	219
UE	Allen's 1271 Third Ave. (at 73rd St.)					○		○			●	242
UW	Allstate Cafe 250 72nd St. (nr. Broadway)			●	○	●		●	○			211
MW	The Angry Squire 216 Seventh Ave. (bt. 22nd and 23rd sts.)	●		○	●	○		●	○		●	120
GV	Arthur's Tavern 57 Grove St. (at Seventh Ave. S.)				●					●		79
MW	Artists and Writers 213 W. 40th St. (at Seventh Ave.)				●				●	●	●	122
DT	The Atrium 100 Washington St. (at Rector St.)				○						●	5
EV	Back East 196 Ave. B (at 12th St.)				●			●	○	●		31
UW	The Balcony 2772 Broadway (at 107th St.)			○		○		●	○			211
DT	Barnabus Rex 155 Duane St. (off W. Broadway)								○	●		25
MW	Barrymore's 267 W. 45th St. (bt. Broadway and Eighth Ave.)									●		141
GV	Benchley's Pub 611 Hudson St. (at 12th St.)			●		○		●			●	55

THE PUBS AT A GLANCE

AREA	NAME & LOCATION	DARTS	GAY	LIT & ART	LIVE ENT.	SINGLES	SPORTS	STUDENTS	THEATER	TRADIT.	LARGE REST.	PAGE NO.
EV	Berry's 180 Spring St. (bt. W. Broadway and Thompson St.)			●				●			●	49
ME	Bill's Gay 90's 57 E. 54th St. (bt. Madison and Park aves.)					●					●	177
ME	Billymunk 302 E. 45th St. (at Second Ave.)					●			●		●	147
ME	Billy's 948 First Ave. (at 53rd St.)									●	●	177
GV	The Bleecker Street 302 Bleecker St. (at Seventh Ave. S.)			●				●			●	56
GV	Bradley's 70 University Pl. (bt. 10th and 11th sts.)			●	●	○	○				●	57
UE	Brandy's I 235 E. 84th St. (bt. Second and Third aves.)					●	●	●				251
ME	Brew's 156 E. 34th St. (bt. Third and Lexington aves.)					●	○	●			●	178
MW	The Briefkase Pub Port Authority Bus Terminal, 2nd floor (41st St. at Eighth Ave.)						●					124
GV	Broadway Charly's 813 Broadway (at 11th St.)					●	●	●	○	●		80
DT	Broker's 46 Gold St. (bt. Fulton and John sts.)	●								●	●	6
GV	Buffalo Roadhouse 87 Seventh Ave. S. (at Barrow St.)			●		○		●	○		●	80
UW	The Café Des Artistes 1 W. 67th St. (nr. Central Park West)			●					○	●	●	192
GR	Caliban 360 Third Ave. (bt. 26th and 27th sts.)			●		●			○		●	93

AREA	NAME & LOCATION	DARTS	GAY	LIT & ART	LIVE ENT.	SINGLES	SPORTS	STUDENTS	THEATER	TRADIT.	LARGE REST.	PAGE NO.
GV	Casey's 142 W. 10th St. (off Greenwich Ave.)	○	○						○		●	81
UE	Catch A Rising Star 1487 First Ave. (at 78th St.)				●	●			●			252
GV	Cedar Tavern 82 University Pl. (bt. 11th and 12th sts.)			●	○	○		●	○		●	58
UW	The Cellar Restaurant 70 W. 95th St. (at Columbus Ave.)				●	○		○			●	193
ME	Charlie Brown's 45th St. (Pan Am Building)					○					●	179
MW	Charlie's 263 W. 45th St. (bt. Broadway and Eighth Ave.)			○					●		●	125
DT	Chateau Tavern 142 Pearl St. (at Wall St.)										●	25
UW	Chipp's Pub 150 Columbus Ave. (at 67th St.)			○		○		○	●		●	212
GV	Chumley's 86 Bedford St. (at Barrow St.)		●	○	○		●	○	●	●	●	60
UE	Churchill's 1277 Third Ave. (bt. 73rd and 74th sts.)					●		●				242
EV	The Colonnades 432 Lafayette St. (at Astor Pl.)		●					●	●		●	33
GR	Company 365 Third Ave. (at 27th St.)	●	○	●					●		●	94
GR	Connelley's 299 Third Ave. (at 23rd St.)								○	●	●	95
ME	Cooney's 152 E. 46th St. (bt. Broadway and Lexington Ave.)			○		○					●	179
UW	Copper Hatch 247 W. 72nd St. (nr. Broadway)			○		○	●	○				213

THE PUBS AT A GLANCE

AREA	NAME & LOCATION	CHARACTERISTICS										PAGE NO.
		DARTS	GAY	LIT & ART	LIVE ENT.	SINGLES	SPORTS	STUDENTS	THEATER	TRADIT.	LARGE REST.	
ME	Costello's 225 E. 44th St. (nr. Third Ave.)			●			○			●	●	149
UE	Daly's Dandelion 1029 Third Ave. (at 61st St.)					●			○	●		221
ME	David Copperfield 322 Lexington Ave. (bt. 38th and 39th sts.)					○					●	180
UW	Dazzels 180 Columbus Ave. (at 68th St.)			○		○		●	●		●	195
GR	Deno's 157 E. 26th St. (at Third Ave.)					○					●	115
ME	Dionysos 304 E. 48th St. (at Second Ave.)			●	●				○		●	151
UE	Don Denton's Pub 154 E. 79th St. (bt. Lexington and Third aves.)					○			○		●	223
MW	Downey's 705 Eighth Ave. (bt. 44th and 45th sts.)			○			○	●	●		●	126
DT	Doyle's Corner Pub 70 Lafayette St. (at Franklin St.)										●	8
UE	Drake's Drum 1629 Second Ave. (bt. 84th and 85th sts.)					○	●	●			●	224
UE	Dr. Generosity 1403 Second Ave. (at 73rd St.)			●	●	●		●	○			225
GV	The Dugout Tavern 145 Bleecker St. (at La Guardia Pl.)					○	○		●	●		82
ME	Duncan's 303 E. 53rd St. (at Second Ave.)					○	●	●			●	153
UE	Elaine's 1703 Second Ave. (at 88th St.)			●					●	●	●	253
DT	Emil's 213 Pearl St. (bt. Maiden Lane and John St.)									●	●	26

AREA	NAME & LOCATION	CHARACTERISTICS										PAGE NO.
		DARTS	GAY	LIT & ART	LIVE ENT.	SINGLES	SPORTS	STUDENTS	THEATER	TRADIT.	LARGE REST.	
NW	The English Pub 900 Seventh Ave. (bt. 56th and 57th sts.)					○			○		●	141
EV	Fanelli's 94 Prince St. (at Mercer St.)			●				●		●	●	35
GV	'55' 55 Christopher St. (at Seventh Ave.)		○	○						●		83
UE	Finnegan's Wake 1361 First Ave. (at 73rd St.)	●				●	●	●			●	254
ME	Fireside Cafe 523 Third Ave. (at 35th St.)									●	●	154
UE	Flanagan's 1215 First Ave. (at 66th St.)			●	●							254
DT	Fraunces Tavern Pearl and Broad sts.									●	●	9
UE	Friday's 1152 First Ave. (at 63rd St.)					●		●			●	227
EV	The Frogpond 414 E. 9th St. (bt. First Ave. and Ave. A)			○				○				50
UW	Ghenghiz Khan's Bicycle 197 Columbus Ave. (at 69th St.)			●	●	●		●	●		●	196
UW	The Ginger Man 51 W. 64th St. (at Broadway)			●		○			●		●	213
MW	Giordano's 409 W. 39th St. (at Ninth Ave.)									●	●	128
UE	Gleason's Tavern 1414 York Ave. (at 75th St.)					●						255
GR	Glocca Morra 304 Third Ave. (at 23rd St.)	●			●	○	●	●				97
UE	Gobbler's Knob 1461 First Ave. (at 76th St.)					●	●	●			●	230
UW	The Gold Rail 2850 Broadway (bt. 110th and 111th sts.)			○		○		●		●	●	198

THE PUBS AT A GLANCE

AREA	NAME & LOCATION	DARTS	GAY	LIT & ART	LIVE ENT.	SINGLES	SPORTS	STUDENTS	THEATER	TRADIT.	LARGE REST.	PAGE NO.
GR	The Good Times 449 Third Ave. (at 31st St.)					○	●	●		○	●	98
ME	The Goose and Gherkin 251 E. 50th St. (at Third Ave.)					○	●			○	●	155
GV	Gottlieb's 343 Bleecker St. (at W. 10th St.)			●		○		●	●		●	62
MW	Great Aunt Fanny's 340 W. 46th St. (bt. Eighth and Ninth aves.)					○				●	●	130
ME	The Green Derby 978 Second Ave. (at 52nd St.)					●	○	●				157
ME	The Green Man 133 E. 56th St. (at Lexington Ave.)	●				○	○	○				158
GR	Greensleeve's 543 Second Ave. (at 30th St.)					○		●			●	100
UE	Gregory's 1149 First Ave. (at 63rd St).					●	○		○			·255
ME	The Guardsman 243 Lexington Ave. (at 34th St.)	●				○	●	○			●	159
GR	Guy Fawke's 365 First Ave. (bt. 21st and 22nd sts.)	●				○	○	●	●			102
ME	Gypsy's 1065 First Ave. (at 58th St.)		●	●					○		●	180
ME	Hanratty's 732 Amsterdam Ave. (at 96th St.)		○		○			●	○		●	199
DT	Harry's At The American Exchange 113 Greenwich St. (at Rector St.)									●	●	10
DT	Harry's At Hanover Square 1 Hanover Square (bt. Pearl and Stone sts.)										●	11
UE	Harry's Back East 1422 Third Ave. (at 81st St.)		●									256

AREA	NAME & LOCATION	CHARACTERISTICS										PAGE NO.
		DARTS	GAY	LIT & ART	LIVE ENT.	SINGLES	SPORTS	STUDENTS	THEATER	TRADIT.	LARGE REST.	
UE	Home 1748 Second Ave. (at 91st St.)				●	●					●	257
GV	Horn of Plenty 91 Charles St. (at Bleecker St.)		○	●					●		●	63
UE	Hudson Bay Inn 1452 Second Ave. (at 76th St.)					●						257
NW	Improvisation 384 W. 44th St. (at Ninth Ave.)			○	●				●			142
ME	Irish Pavilion 130 E. 57th St. (bt. Lexington and Park aves.)				●	○					●	181
GV	Jacques At The Village Corner 142 Bleecker St. (at La Guardia Pl.)	●		●	●	○	○	●				64
UE	J. G. Melon 1291 Third Ave. (at 74th St.)				●		●			●		241
MW	Jilly's 256 W. 52nd St. (at Eighth Ave.)				●					○	●	142
GV	Jimmy Day's 192 W. 4th St. (bt. Sixth and Seventh aves.)		○			○	●	●			●	66
MW	Jimmy Ray's 729 Eighth Ave. (bt. 45th and 46th sts.)								●			132
MW	Jimmy Ryan's 154 W. 54th St. (bt. Sixth and Seventh aves.)				●					●		143
MW	Joe Allen 326 W. 46th St. (bt. Eighth and Ninth aves.)		○						●		●	143
ME	The John Barleycorn 209 E. 45th St. (nr. Third Ave.)				●	○	○				●	161
DT	The Jolly Monk 59 Warren St. (at W. Broadway)	●										26

AREA	NAME & LOCATION	CHARACTERISTICS										PAGE NO.
		DARTS	GAY	LIT & ART	LIVE ENT.	SINGLES	SPORTS	STUDENTS	THEATER	TRADIT.	LARGE REST.	
UE	J.P.'s 1471 First Ave. (bt. 76th and 77th sts.)		○	●	○				●		●	258
GV	Julius 159 W. 10th St. (at Waverly Pl.)	●	○				○					67
EV	Kenn's Broome Street Bar 363 W. Broadway (at Broome St.)			●		○		●				37
GR	Kenwall 129 Lexington Ave. (bt. 28th and 29th sts.)									●		115
ME	Kitty Hawk's 565 Third Ave. (at 37th St.)					●		●			●	162
EV	Kiwi II 432 E. 9th St. (bt. Ave. A and First Ave.)			○				○				39
ME	Knickers 928 Second Ave. (at 49th St.)					○			○		●	163
EV	Lady Astor's 430 Lafayette St. (at Astor Pl.)			●		○		○	●		●	50
MW	Landmark Tavern 46th St. (at Eleventh Ave.)			○		○			●			133
UW	The Library 2475 Broadway (at 92nd St.)			●		○		●	○		●	200
GR	Limerick's 573 Second Ave. (at 31st St.)			○		○					●	103
GV	The Lion's Head 59 Christopher St. (at Seventh Ave.)			●		○		○		●	●	69
UE	Lion's Rock 316 E. 77th St. (bt. Second and Third aves.)					●					●	258
GV	The Locale 11 Waverly Pl. (at Mercer St.)			●		○		●	●			83
EV	Lüchows 110 E. 14th St. (at Irving Pl.)			●						●	●	51

AREA	NAME & LOCATION	CHARACTERISTICS										PAGE NO.
		DARTS	GAY	LIT & ART	LIVE ENT.	SINGLES	SPORTS	STUDENTS	THEATER	TRADIT.	LARGE REST.	
NW	Ma Bell's 218 W. 45th St. (at Shubert Alley)								●			135
UE	The Mad Hatter 1485 Second Ave. (at 77th St.)					●	●				●	233
UE	Martell's 1489 Third Ave. (at 83rd St.)			○	○			○	●	●	●	235
ME	Maude's Summit Hotel (51st St. and Lexington Ave.)					●					●	181
UE	Maxwell's Plum 1181 First Ave. (at 61st St.)			●		●			●		●	237
UW	McGlade's 154 Columbus Ave. (at 67th St.)			○					○	●	●	214
UE	McMaster's 413 71st St. (bt. York and First aves.)					●	●		●		●	239
EV	McSorley's 15 E. 7th St. (nr. Third Ave.)			●				●	●	●		40
ME	Michael's Pub 919 Third Ave. (at 55th St.)					●	●		●		●	165
DT	Michael's 2 10 Hanover Square (at Pearl St.)										●	27
UW	Mikell's 760 Columbus Ave. (at 97th St.)			○	●			●	○		●	202
GV	Minetta Tavern 113 MacDougal St. (at Minetta Lane)			○							●	84
GR	Molly Malone's 287 Third Ave. (bt. 22nd and 23rd sts.)	●			○		●	○	●	●	●	104
ME	Monk's Court 244 E. 51st St. (at Second Ave.)										●	182
DT	Morgan's 134 Read St. (bt. Hudson and Greenwich sts.)					○					●	27

AREA	NAME & LOCATION	CHARACTERISTICS										PAGE NO.
		DARTS	GAY	LIT & ART	LIVE ENT.	SINGLES	SPORTS	STUDENTS	THEATER	TRADIT.	LARGE REST.	
UW	Mrs. J's Sacred Cow 228 W. 72nd St. (nr. Broadway)			●	●				●	●	●	214
UE	Mugg's 1134 First Ave. (bt. 62nd and 63rd sts.)				●	○					●	240
GR	Munk's Park 379 Park Ave. S. (bt. 26th and 27th sts.)				○						●	115
UW	The Music Room 2871 Broadway (bt. 111th and 112th sts.)			●	●			●	●		●	203
UE	My House 1160 First Ave. (at 63rd St.)				●	○		○			●	259
GV	No-Name Bar 621 Hudson St. (at Jane St.)				●			●	●			70
ME	O'Casey's 108 E. 41st St. (bt. Lexington and Park aves.)						○				●	182
GR	Old Town 45 E. 18th St. (bt. Park Ave. S. and Broadway)									●		116
ME	O'Lunney's 915 Second Ave. (bt. 48th and 49th sts.)					●	○	●			●	183
UW	O'Neals' Baloon 48th W. 63rd St. (at Columbus Ave.)				○			●	●		●	205
UW	O'Neal Bros. 269 Columbus Ave. (at 72nd St.)	●		●		●		●	●			215
GR	Once Upon A Stove 325 Third Ave. (at 24th St.)					●	○			○	●	105
GV	1 If By Land, 2 If By Sea 17 Barrow St. (bt. W. 4th St. and Seventh Ave.)		○	●	○	●			●		●	71
EV	162 Spring Street 162 Spring St. (at W. Broadway)				●	○		●	●		●	52
EV	Orchidia 145 Second Ave. (at 9th St.)			○				●	●		●	42

AREA	NAME & LOCATION	CHARACTERISTICS										PAGE NO.
		DARTS	GAY	LIT & ART	LIVE ENT.	SINGLES	SPORTS	STUDENTS	THEATER	TRADIT.	LARGE REST.	
GV	The Other End 149 Bleecker St. (at La Guardia Pl.)				●	●		●			●	73
ME	Oyster Bar Grand Central Terminal (42nd St.)					○				●	●	179
DT	Paris Bar 119 South St. (at Peck Slip)									●		16
UE	Patch's Inn 314 E. 70th St. (bt. First and Second aves.)				●	○					●	243
ME	Peartrees 1 Mitchell Pl. (First Ave. and 49th St.)					●					●	166
UE	Pedro's 251 E. 85th St. (at Second Ave.)			○		○			○	●		260
ME	Pen and Pencil 205 E. 45th St. (nr. Third Ave.)			○			○		○	●	●	183
GV	Peter's Backyard 64 W. 10th St. (at Sixth Ave.)			○					○		●	84
GR	Pete's Tavern 129 E. 18th St. (at Irving Pl.)					○	○			●	●	107
EV	Phebe's 361 Bowery (at 4th St.)			○				●	●		●	43
ME	P.J. Clarke's 915 Third Ave. (at 55th St.)			●		●	●		●	●	●	168
UE	P.J. Moriarty 1034 Third Ave. (at 61st St.)										●	244
UW	P.S. 77 355 Amsterdam Ave. (at 77th St.)			●	●				●		●	215
UE	The Recovery Room 417 E. 70th St. (bt. First and York aves.)					●		●			●	245
UE	The Red Blazer 1571 Second Ave. (bt. 81st and 82nd sts.)					●	●				●	246

THE PUBS AT A GLANCE

AREA	NAME & LOCATION	DARTS	GAY	LIT & ART	LIVE ENT.	SINGLES	SPORTS	STUDENTS	THEATER	TRADIT.	LARGE REST.	PAGE NO.
ME	The Reidy's 22 E. 54th St. (bt. Fifth and Madison aves.)			○					○	●	●	170
MW	R.J. Scotty's 202 Ninth Ave. (bt. 22nd and 23rd sts.)								○		●	136
DT	Rosie O'Grady's South 211 Pearl St. (bt. Maiden Lane and John St.)					●	○					13
ME	Rumm's Tavern 208 E. 50th St. (nr. Third Ave.)						●		○			171
DT	St. Charlie's 4 Albany St. (at Washington St.)					○	○				●	14
GV	St. James' Infirmary 22 Seventh Ave. S. (at Leroy St.)			○	●			●	○			85
GV	The Sazerac House 533 Hudson St. (at Charles St.)			●				●		●	●	75
ME	Scoop 210 E. 43rd St. (bt. Second and Third aves.)			●					○		●	184
UE	September's 1442 First Ave. (at 75th St.)					○	●	●				260
DT	Sketch Pad 91 South St. (at Fulton St.)			○				○			●	16
DT	Smitty's 5 Gold St. (bt. John St. and Maiden Lane)					○					●	18
EV	Soho Darts Bar 60 Mercer St. (at Broome St.)	●		●		○		●				45
DT	Square Rigger Fulton and Front sts.									●		16
UW	Stryker's 103 W. 86th St. (at Columbus Ave.)			○	●	○		●	○			216

AREA	NAME & LOCATION	DARTS	GAY	LIT & ART	LIVE ENT.	SINGLES	SPORTS	STUDENTS	THEATER	TRADIT.	LARGE REST.	PAGE NO.
GV	Sweet Basil 88 Seventh Ave. S. (bt. Grove and Bleecker sts.)			●	●	○		●			●	77
UW	Teacher's 2249 Broadway (bt. 80th and 81st sts.)			○		○			○		●	206
ME	The Three Farthings 111 E. 40th St. (bt. Park and Lexington aves.)					○				●	●	173
ME	Three Lions Pub 304 E. 42nd St. (bt. First and Second aves.)					○						185
MW	Thursday's 57 W. 58th St. (bt. Fifth and Sixth aves.)						●	○	○		●	137
GR	Timothy's Winery 127 Lexington Ave. (bt. 28th and 29th sts.)						○	○	○		●	109
EV	Tin Palace 325 Bowery (at Second St.)			●	●	○		●	●			46
MW	Tripple Inn 263 W. 54th St. (bt. Broadway and Eighth Ave.)	●				●		●	●			144
GR	Tuesday's 190 Third Ave. (at 17th St.)						○	●			●	111
ME	Uncle Charlie's South 581 Third Ave. (at 38th St.)		●									175
UE	Waltzing Matilda 1567 Second Ave. (bt. 81st and 82nd sts.)	●					○	●	○		●	247
MW	West Boondock 114 Tenth Ave. (at 17th St.)				●	○			○		●	138
UW	The West End 2911 Broadway (bt. 113th and 114th sts.)			●	●	○		●		●	●	207
GV	The White Horse Tavern 567 Hudson St. (at 11th St.)			○				●		●		87

THE PUBS AT A GLANCE

AREA	NAME & LOCATION	CHARACTERISTICS										PAGE NO.
		DARTS	GAY	LIT & ART	LIVE ENT.	SINGLES	SPORTS	STUDENTS	THEATER	TRADIT.	LARGE REST.	
GV	William Shakespeare's 176 MacDougal St. (at Eighth St.)			○	○	○		●			●	88
UE	Willie's 1426 Third Ave. (at 81st St.)					○				●	●	248
DT	Willy's 186 William St. (at Beekman St.)									●	●	19
DT	Ye Olde Chop House 111 Broadway (near Wall St.)									●	●	21
DT	Ye Olde Dutch Tavern 15 John St. (bt. Broadway and Nassau St.)									●	●	22